# Aquaponics in a Changing World...

## Introducing the *Aqua-Pod*

By Jim Gibson

CRA Independent Publishing | Tampa. FL

First CRA publishing June 2015.

ISBN - 13: 978-1515137504    ISBN - 10: 1515137503

UUID:3287620d-beb1-418f-8875-d1e8ba26faee

Print publisher enquiries welcomed at aqua.podcra@gmail.com.

# Aquaponics in a Changing World… Introducing the *Aqua-Pod*

Jim Gibson

*Become a Part of Positive Change! Grow Food in a Sustainable Manner and Become an Active Member of the Aquaponics Community of Concerned Farmers.*
\*\*\*

*The DIY Enthusiast's Guide to Growing Vegetables and Fish Together at Home or On the Farm!*
\*\*\*

*Build Your Own High-Output Food System! Interior - Greenhouse & Artificial Lighting - and Exterior Operations.*
\*\*\*

Food security at home and abroad is one of the most pressing issues of our time. The rapidly increasing effects of global climate change and the decreasing availability of water and fossil fuels are together projected to exert tremendous downward pressure on our global food supply. Current industrialized agriculture is contributing to the issue with excessive use of synthetic fertilizers, pesticides and herbicides. Farming techniques, as we know them today, will become obsolete as the Earth's resources continue to dwindle. The development of aquaponics, a proven sustainable system for efficiently and symbiotically growing vegetables and fish together, may be one of the most important scientific and social innovations of the 21st century.

Take the guesswork out of sustainable gardening with this hands-on construction & operations manual to growing vegetables and fish together.

*Aquaponics in a Changing World… Introducing the Aqua-Pod* provides step-by-step detailed instructions for constructing a small-scale, highly efficient backyard or interior – greenhouse or artificial lighting - aquaponic farm. Complete plans are combined with an introduction to the benefits of this exciting technology, tips for selecting plants and aquatic life, and detailed installation and maintenance instructions. Start small and grow your operation to any size to fit your needs.

Unlike most of the books currently on the market which tend to offer a broad overview of the technique, this hands-on, practical, concise manual provides everything you need to know to get the *Aqua-Pod* system up and running. Complete plans are combined with an introduction to the benefits of this exciting technology, tips for selecting plants and aquatic life, and detailed installation and maintenance instructions.

As the community and culture continue to move away from social democracy – one person/one vote – and towards capital manipulation – wealth devised government; aquaponics provides the individual, the family and the community control over the most basic needs - food and nourishment for ourselves and our children. There can be little debate about the fact our foods are being manipulated to provide excessive profits for a very few. Aquaponics "levels" the field is many ways.

**What people are saying about "Aquaponics in a Changing World... Introducing the *Aqua-Pod"*...**

*"Finally! A complete system I was able to assemble and produce food for my family. No gimmicks... just results!"*
***

"Very detailed instructions with the kind of background information required for success."

***

*"We had several questions throughout the process. We received immediate responses and even photographs and, in one case, a drawing to help us. We aren't what you would call 'seasoned' builders and designers but with the detailed manual and a couple 'shout-outs' we are growing great tasting food and fat, happy fish."*

\*\*\*

"Like any well developed and successful concept the devil is in the details. The *Aqua-Pod,* with 216 base 'pots' randomly changed-out and renewed, provides required system strength and balance. The bio-filter strength is unprecedented."

\*\*\*

*"The combination of Aquaponics and soil-based growth creates an abundance of food of just about any variety desired using a small area of operation. The increased production, requiring just 6% of the water used in industrial agriculture for the same returns, is a great option and even better when considering the plants receive the full required nitrates for healthy, full growth."*

\*\*\*

"There is a lot 'out there' when it comes to aquaponics but nothing I can find that details a working system like this. 'A' to 'Z' instructions to put your own *Aqua-Pod* to work for you, your family and community."

\*\*\*

*"A fool proof design. No 'siphons' or 'fill and drain' gizmo's. No waking up to find your ponds drained and empty (and your fish dead!). Nothing involved that can't be purchased in a hardware or pet store. A system so simple and durable all that needs done is to pick your seed and grow! And when you come right down to it... that's what gardening is all about."*

\*\*\*

"I use the *Aqua-Pod* for interior artificial light growth and it's great. The results are a much smoother taste and flavor without the harshness I get with hydroponic additives. Potent yet smooth tasting... a quality natural product!"

\*\*\*

*"Living in a northern climate, we operate as a greenhouse throughout the year. What's great about the Aqua-Pod is with a little planning we can have strong seedlings ready to put in immediately when the weather moderates. We run crops three to six weeks ahead of our neighbors and are often able to get two rounds of some crops per summer season."*

\*\*\*

"The *Aqua-Pod* really caught our eye and we were quite interested. We contacted CRA and asked if they offer classes and the cost. You can imagine our excitement when told there were no costs to come down and spend time at CRA. It took just two days to "walk" through the processes described in the manual. We now have two *Aqua-Pods* and are considering installing two more. The *Aqua-Pod* design is a pleasure to work with and we are growing a lot of different foods throughout the year and have many fat, happy fish!"

\*\*\*

*Creating food with fish poop isn't all that attractive to the uneducated – both those uneducated regarding the science of aquaponics and those uneducated about the methods of production of their current food stream. I am certain - I repeat – I am certain that aquaponic production will not only become viable but that it may be one of the most important scientific and social innovations of the 21st century. If I am over passionate, please forgive me, but I suggest that aquaponic technology may well feed the human race at some point in the not too distant future. In 2008, when I entered into aquaponic research & development I was of the belief aquaponics would achieve a solid footing worldwide in 50 to 75 years. I now suspect it will be a major component of vegetable and protein production in the next 15 to 25 years. It will depend on the weather and the rapidly increasing affects of global climate change and the decreasing availability of water and fossil fuels. It will also depend on whether we know the process and can deliver on it. We must teach ourselves and our children these methods and our children must pass this knowledge to all for all times.*

# FORWARD

*Harvest Bounty*

"**Those who profess to favor freedom and yet depreciate agitation are people who want crops without plowing the ground; they want rain without thunder and lightning; they want the ocean without the roar of its many waters. The struggle may be a moral one, or it may be a physical one, or it may be both. But it must be a struggle. Power concedes nothing without a demand. It never did and it never will.**"

*Frederick Douglas, 1857*

The above was my second to final response to a publisher "excited" to publish this book.

"**This manual is anything but a 'Martha Stewart' coffee table curio and will not be published as such under any circumstance what so ever.**"

*Jim Gibson, February 2015*

That was my final statement after receiving the publisher's "edited" version with some 36% removed because *"the reader probably doesn't want to be confronted with the issues we have chosen to delete"*.

*Well… aquaponics starts with the raising of fish and plants as a food source. That can't be disputed. But, there is much more involved in aquaponics that includes food justice, community self-determination and the ecological balance of a planet currently being stressed beyond its means.*

*Look… these are important issues that we, as a civilization, need to deal with. Maybe it makes some of us uncomfortable to consider but it's a fact… we are destroying the planet upon which we live and survive. Aquaponics offers a solution to many of the conditions faced through the process of big industrialized agriculture. If the reader, to this point of the narrative, finds that they "don't want to be confronted" with the discussion herein then, by all means, don't waste your time with "Aquaponics in a Changing World".*

Let's visit several facts about aquaponics:

1. **Big Industrial Agriculture doesn't like aquaponic methods and are going to do all they can to discourage the growth of the aquaponic community.** Big Ag is huge and it means big money. From the manufacture of industrial fertilizers, pesticides and herbicides to the planting, watering, raising, harvesting and delivery of the crops there are big, very big, profits made. From the petroleum and gas industry to the fertilizer and pesticide industry the

resistance to aquaponics, which use little to none of these resources, will increase as aquaponics becomes more widely researched, developed and placed into operation. Monsanto, Cargill, Mosaic, Bayer, Exxon, BP, Scott's and Koch have sustainable farming in their headlights and as the most sustainable of all methods, aquaponics, takes hold there will be greater resistance developed and applied from such financially well-healed and politically savvy opponents.

2. **Aquaponics does not, can not, and never will "compete" with Big Industrial Agriculture.** Furthermore there is no reason to even consider competition with an industry that produces a grossly inferior product. A tomato grown by Big Ag and a tomato grown aquaponically are two distinct and different products and as aquaponics takes hold throughout the world people will see and accept this. The Big Ag GMO tomato, produced with industrially manufactured fertilizers and pesticides and grown with copious amounts of water and the excessive use of polluting petroleum products, isn't "food" and it is harmful to those who eat it on a regular basis. In the USA, as of late, there has been great concern about child vaccinations and the possible effects they might have on our young. I would suggest we would be better served to protect our kids from Big Ag "food" products if we want to see a decrease in instances of "autism", food allergies and obesity. If people want to be healthy, and remain that way, they need to eat real food grown in a healthy manner.

3. **Aquaponics provides for control of our food by the individual operator/gardener.** As the community and culture continue to move away from social democracy – one person/one vote – and towards capital manipulation – wealth devised government - we will experience a further disconnect in "truth in marketing" where we

will soon be unable to discern the quality and make-up of industrially produced and marketed "foods". This is already evident where there is no requirement (in the USA) that GMO foods be labeled as such. We can also see the affects of this type of "deregulation" in the gas and oil fracking process where the chemical make-up of injected fluids remain "proprietary" secrets while those living within areas with active wells find their water unsafe, tainted and, in a number of cases, flammable; without the ability to challenge the drillers to divulge the toxins used. It's the same with our food stream. We don't know what the genetic make-up of a GMO tomato is because it's "proprietary". Sure it looks "red" and it seems chewable and sliceable. But is it really food that the human body is meant to process?

4. **Aquaponics is an honest food source and a truly organic product.** The aquaponics farmer can't "cook" the books to make it appear the process is "organic". Industrial fertilizers, pesticides and herbicides cannot be used in aquaponics… *the fish will die*. While it may take a considerable amount of time and effort to "certify" a conventional "organic" farm operation, an aquaponics farm can be declared organic in one simple pass by examining the fish and their physical well-being. I might suggest that General Foods and Kellogg's (and the multitude of other "food" manufacturers) will be much challenged to rush out and declare their products "organic" (as they have done previously) if the requirements were as strenuous as required by aquaponics and the well-being of the fish.

I urge the reader to look further into this publication by reading the "introduction" that follows. In the "introduction" I discuss the theory and basis of this manual and describe in general the actual development, construction and operation of a successful aquaponics garden. It is then up to the reader to commit to further proceed with their own aquaponics operation and all that it means to the community and the Earth as a whole. Good luck!

### About the Design and Digital Conversion of this Book

*If you are anything like myself – old and crusty – you probably spent from age 10 on with a paperback book or two stuffed in your back pocket or jammed into a pack or purse. Well… times are changing and, though I have to admit I enjoy the feel, smell and action of turning pages, dog-earing the corners and having a margin to scribble the occasional comment - digital books are a reality and the wave of the future.*

*Upon severing my contract with an established publishing house I was confronted with the reality of getting this book to "press". I had always coveted the option of publishing digitally. As a matter of fact I had tried very hard to maintain the rights to digital publication – giving the un-named publishing house full "print" rights - but to no avail.*

*So… with my new found freedom to develop and create my own digital book I was, needless to say, rather excited. Problem was - I didn't have the slightest idea how to go about creating a digital book. Fortunately we live with one of the greatest inventions of our time (and perhaps all times) – the wonderful world of the internet. If one wants to figure out how to do something it can be discovered somewhere, somehow on the internet.*

*To make a long story short, it took me about six weeks to compile the material and raise the first ".epub" to be viewed and edited in a digital format. The simple reality of the ".epub" format is that it is based on web page principles and digital books don't read exactly like what an old crusty fart like me would expect. Though there are a number of programs available that can "cobble" a digital book together, they are primarily designed for fiction publications and they do not render a "technical manual", such as this book, well.*

*I'm not going to bore the reader discussing "metadata", "xhtml", "xml",*

*".epub", ".mobi", ".opf", "META-INF", "OEBPS", ".ncx", ".css" or the myriad of styles, programs and requirements to build a digital book except to say –"Aquaponics in a Changing World" is what is referred to as a "hand coded" publication. To get an end product acceptable to ME it required that I build the book from scratch without the use of any outside software.*

*Having said the preceding – "fessed-up" so to speak – I'm not quite sure I should admit to my endeavor except to repeat - the book meets my own demands for a sound production where the user of this manual can fully understand the process, follow the process and complete the process as defined within.*

*Though I have reviewed this book on a number of digital reading platforms I want to emphasize that I have not viewed the book on every platform. It is also important for the reader to understand that I have gone to great lengths so that those without the most sophisticated digital readers (those in third world countries – where this information is vitally important) can easily view and use the information contained.*

*"Open sourced" – .epub – production capability is perhaps one of the most important and "democratizing" innovations of our time. With this technology anyone and everyone has the ability and freedom to express themselves in the most powerful of all mediums – the written word.*

**True, This! - Beneath the rule of men entirely great - The pen is mightier than the sword!**

# CONTENTS

# I. INTRODUCTION

Google "aquaponics" and you will return some 1.2(+) million hits. Though I've sampled fewer than 500 sites, the vast majority want to sell the visitor some item or another. Many don't really have much to sell that one cannot make or contrive oneself, and many have not – in truth – realized the successes they often claim.

The material you are about to visit herein has nothing – and has never had anything – to do with making money. The information contained in this text has been solely developed, designed, implemented and researched at the Cyrson Ranch Aquaponic Research and Development center in Tampa Bay, Florida. It remains my intention that anyone anywhere can obtain this book and work with it. It has taken close to seven years to arrive at the point where we, at Cyrson Aquaponics Ranch R&D, are confident of the design and success of the aquaponics platform – the *Aqua-Pod* - and related aquaponic techniques and farm/garden. If you are interested in the construction and operation of a nutritional film technique (NFT) aquaponics and related hybrid garden, this text provides a detailed map and it is a valuable tool to achieve success.

With this book you will be able to construct and operate a Nutrient Film Technique (NFT) aquaponics system – the *Aqua-Pod* – successfully and incorporate this system into a productive hybrid garden operation.

All of the items used in construction of the *Aqua-Pod* and related hybrid garden are "off-the-shelf" components, and any "modified" component requirements are carefully discussed and illustrated so you can make these modifications yourself.

I discuss the operational mechanical plant and the installation of peripherals; such as fluid-transfer piping and pumps, water storage and conditioning, and aquaponically fed hybrid soil-based crops installations, and how they fit into a well-rounded operation. I discuss farm layout techniques and time-saving tips.

I discuss the husbandry of animals (fish) and the balance between these creatures' requirements and the successful growth of crops and other vegetation. I discuss analysis techniques and corrections required. I also discuss and guide the reader in the most important aspect of successful aquaponics – the creation and maintenance of the *bio-filter*. You will be guided by our initial – and continuing – commitment to *zero tolerance for the reckless destruction of the aquaculture.*

I include our original mission statement that was developed in 2008 and guides all that we at Cyrson Ranch Aquaponics R&D have accomplished and continue to accomplish. This manual, and those to follow, addresses *"Aquaponics in a Changing World"*. We simply must develop food sources that reduce the reliance on fossil fuels, excessive water consumption and harmful pesticides and herbicides. We must create food streams that mitigate destructive industrial Big Ag techniques and expand local sourcing and control of our community's food. With this in mind I point out, throughout this manual, numerous instances where our environment and our food sources are being manipulated, compromised and destroyed to financially enrich a very small number of people. Aquaponics cannot be discussed without the addition of this very important, and often contentious, analysis.

The *Aqua-Pod* has proven all that was expected when the initial design was implemented. The *Aqua-Pod* is quite reliable and easy to work with. The system attributes ensure a strong over-all environment for both the fish and plants. Working the 216 individual system "pots" and the constant renewal of the bio-filter reservoir make a filter collapse nearly impossible if not altogether so. The quality and quantity of food generated in such a small physical package make the *Aqua-Pod* and garden very attractive to both the gardener and the larger scale operator. Finally, the *Aqua-Pod* is a great platform to train people in the field of aquaponics and to research and communicate with one another throughout the globe.

## II. HOW TO USE THIS MANUAL

*With the advent of the motor car it was not until the Ford Motor Company produced the Model "T" in mass that the automobile was eventually understood and embraced by the world as a whole. We here at CRA like to think of the Aqua-Pod as the "Tin Lizzy" of aquaponics.*

This manual is written to expose the reader to the application of aquaponics as a sustainable food source. The material provides the reader with a proven aquaponic platform – the *Aqua-Pod* - and hybrid garden to explore and the opportunity to develop an intimate understanding of this very important science.

*It has been our intention at CRA to design, build and create an aquaponics platform that brings the science to the world community as a whole. We do not assume the Aqua-Pod to be the most efficient production platform in aquaponics nor do we believe – at this time –*

*that any such system has yet been developed. The Aqua-Pod offers simplicity, durability and proven operational integrity. The Aqua-Pod platform is extremely flexible and very forgiving of mistakes and when certain conditions are missed or overlooked.*

For the most part, *Aquaponics in a Changing World* is a technical manual. You will be guided through the definition and history of aquaponics and its various methods, the construction of the *Aqua-Pod* platform, the selection of vegetation and aquatic life, the science of the bio-filter creation and the installation and maintenance of an aquaponically fed hybrid garden. Every effort has been made to visit the many pitfalls and issues encountered over the past 7(+) years of research and development so that you, as a user of this manual, can build the *Aqua-Pod*, install the aquaponically fed soil-based hybrid garden and hit the track running.

*Aquaponics in a Changing World* is written to educate and to assist those who educate others. At the end of the manual there is a question-and-answer follow-up for each section. Some questions cover the most basic elements: measuring, safety, tool identification and operations while others visit topics concerning a *changing world*: diminishing fuels and water supplies; genetically modified organisms (GMOs); and pesticides, herbicides and synthetic fertilizers and their effect on food production, the environment and the future of the planet Earth. These questions offer the educator the chance to draw students into important discussions and enhance the learning process.

As an engineering officer aboard merchant vessels I have, for over 30 years, used technical manuals on a daily basis and I suggest this proven method: Sit down with *Aquaponics in a Changing World* and initially scan the information. Don't focus on any one area – rather take the time to find out where the information is located within the manual. When you get into the "nuts and bolts" of your own *Aqua-Pod* and hybrid garden operation, you will have a good idea of where you need to go in the manual when it's necessary.

Using *Aquaponics in a Changing World* as a manual, as intended, you will find yourself concentrated within sections at various times and may well find you refer to several sections on a regular, or seasonal, basis. It is for that reason that I have included many of the basics – the *why's* and *how's* of sustainable aquaponics – a number of times throughout the manual. Many, most, of these points are *"tinted"* within a colored boundary. Though, at first glance, this may appear repetitive, that is not the intent. Keeping a mind to the basics helps to inspire, guide and educate the aquaponics operator and gardener to achieve their goals and experience success.

Every attempt has been made to address any issue that may arise and a FAQ/troubleshooting section is attached toward the end of the manual. The simple reality is that questions will always come up that the manual hasn't addressed. It is my intention that this manual be issued as a new edition on a yearly basis or as required. Please do not hesitate to contact me with any questions, suggestions or edits.

I can be reached at *aqua.podcra@ gmail. com.* We, at CRA, are available to help you.

*Lettuce Growing in the Aqua-Pod*

*Flowers Growing in the Aqua-Pod*

*Creating food with fish poop isn't all that attractive to the uneducated – both those uneducated regarding the science of aquaponics and those uneducated about the methods of production of their current food stream. I am certain - I repeat – I am certain* *that aquaponic production will not only become viable but that it may be one of the most important scientific and social innovations of the 21st century. If I am over passionate, please forgive me, but I suggest that aquaponic technology may well feed the human race at some point in the not too distant future. In 2008, when I entered into aquaponic research & development I was of the belief aquaponics would achieve a solid footing worldwide in 50 to 75 years. I now suspect it will be a major component of vegetable and protein production in the next 15 to 25 years. It will depend on the weather and the rapidly increasing affects of global climate change and the decreasing availability of water and fossil fuels. It will also depend on whether **we** know the process and can deliver on it. We **must** teach ourselves and our children these methods and our children **must** leave this knowledge to all for all times.*

### *Suggested Best Viewing Practices of a Technical Digital Publication*

*As mentioned previously there are several idiosyncrasies in using, and viewing, a digital publication and it's good to take a moment to discuss some options available to the user of a technical manual such as this one.*

*Technical books are best viewed by "scrolling" down through the material where one is able, when necessary, to "track back" and closely view both the written material and any desired accompanying images, tables or pictures. Most "readers" offer a scroll option that the user can select and use.*

*There are numerous cloud applications available to the public at no cost to download to a pad or PC. Though I've tested this book on a number of these offerings, for .epub files using cloud technology, I have found Google*

*Skood and the FB Reader to be the best of many offered (though I haven't come anywhere near testing all that's out there!).*

*If you arrived at this book through Amazon you may be reading a .kpf file in a "fixed" format. A fixed format doesn't render as many "reader" options (font selection and size) so if you are having difficulty with the manual contact me and I'll send you the ".mobi" file you can use on a PC, MAC or your personal reader.*

*It's best, if possible, to download this, and any book, to a PC or MAC where a file with the extension ".epub", ".mobi" and the like is created. From there you can open your book on any number of free software applications. Reading on my PC I use, for ".epub" files, Adobe "Digital Editions" and, for ".mobi" files, I use the Kindle "Reader". And finally... by downloading a book to a PC file one now has the freedom to "cross-load" (or email the file) the book to any number of "pad" readers and taken where ever desired and read.*

## III. AQUAPONICS DEFINED

It is important that the reader and potential operator of the *Aqua-Pod* and related soil-based hybrid garden become familiar with the history and scientific realities of aquaponics. I urge you to seek out as much information as possible. An excellent place to start learning is through the Wikipedia outlet and then branch out – through various sources – to develop a greater depth of knowledge to assist in the creation of your *Aqua-Pod* and hybrid garden; daily operations, farm growth, troubleshooting and any required corrections.

The Oxford Dictionary defines aquaponics as

"A system of aquaculture in which the waste produced by farmed fish or other aquatic animals supplies nutrients for plants grown hydroponically, which in turn purify the water."

That definition is exact, but if aquaponics were really as simple as that I could have put it on a post card, stamped it, sent it out and put myself out of my misery long ago. Unfortunately aquaponics is not that simple.

### A General Description of Aquaponics

Aquaponics is a food-production system that combines conventional aquaculture (raising aquatic animals such as snails, fish, crayfish or prawns in tanks) with hydroponics (cultivating plants in water) in a symbiotic environment. In normal aquaculture, excretions from the animals being raised can accumulate in the water, increasing toxicity. In an aquaponic system, water from an aquaculture system is fed into a hydroponic system where nitrogen-fixing bacteria break down the by-products into nitrites and nitrates, which the plants use as nutrients. The water is then recirculated to the aquaculture system, and the process starts over again.

As existing hydroponic and aquaculture farming techniques form the basis for all aquaponics systems, the size, complexity, and types of foods grown in an aquaponics system can vary as much as those found in the use of the two methods – hydroponics and aquaponics - separately. Perhaps the one limiting factor required is that aquaponics must utilize fresh water aquacultures and, for the most part, saltwater species cannot be considered.

The exact history of aquaponics is sketchy, but it has been suggested that it was viable source of vegetables and proteins in ancient times and was used along the Nile River, in China and by the Aztec culture in the Central and South Americas.

**Aquaponics Today**

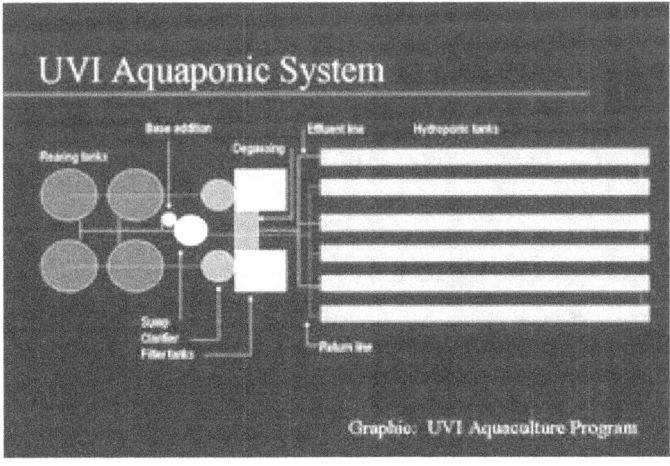

*The University of the Virgin Islands Aquaponics Farm*

Recent development of aquaponics has occurred throughout the world involving individuals, academia, community groups and organizations, and various non-profit entities. There is a growing wealth of information and support through online forums that discuss current systems, issues and the international development of aquaponics.

Aquaponic components are simple: The pump removes the effluent from the fish tank/ponds and injects it into media beds, tubes or floating rafts in trays. Other components involved are the sump and filter. Plant growth can be accomplished in several manners:

*Credit - Aquaponics with Catfish by Ryan Somma-Aquaponics*

- Deep-water raft aquaponics: Styrofoam rafts floating in relatively deep aquaculture basins or "troughs" hold the plants with roots exposed to nutrients.
- Recirculating aquaponics: Solid media, such as gravel or clay beads, are held in a container that is flooded with water from the aquaculture. This type of aquaponics is also known as closed-loop aquaponics.

- Reciprocating aquaponics: Solid media in a container is alternately flooded and drained, using different types of siphon drains. This type of aquaponics is also known as flood-and-drain aquaponics or ebb-and-flow aquaponics.
- Other systems use towers that are trickle-fed from the top, nutrient film technique channels, horizontal PVC pipes with holes for the pots, or plastic barrels cut in half with gravel or rafts in them. Each approach has its own benefits and possible detractions dependent on design.

Aquatic life in aquaponics is most commonly fish of various species, although freshwater crayfish and prawns are sometimes used. Though tilapia is possibly the most commonly used fish, other varieties have been used, including barramundi, silver perch, eel-tailed catfish or tandanus catfish, jade perch and Murray cod. Not all locales permit all types of fish due to restrictions preventing invasive species. In Florida (the location of Cyrson Ranch Aquaponics R&D) the only accepted tilapia is the blue tilapia.

Fish Poop to Fertilizer – How It Works

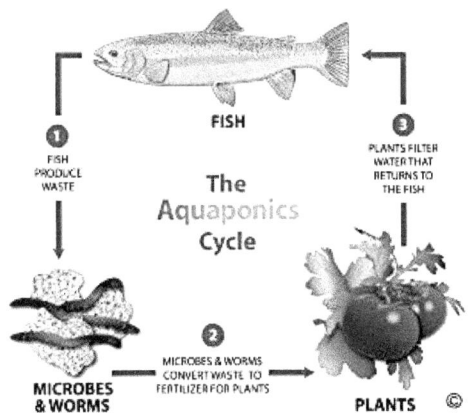

*Graphics Credit - TheAquaponicsSource.com*

Nitrification, the aerobic (using "oxygen" as opposed to "anaerobic" - oxygen free) conversion of ammonia into nitrates, is one of the most important functions in an aquaponics system as it reduces the toxicity of the water for fish and allows the resulting nitrate compounds to be removed by the plants as nourishment. Ammonia is steadily released into the water through the excreta and gills of fish as a product of their metabolism. It must be filtered out of the water because high concentrations of ammonia will kill fish. Although plants can absorb ammonia from the water to some degree, they assimilate nitrates more easily, thereby efficiently reducing the toxicity of the water. Ammonia can be converted into other nitrogenous compounds through healthy populations of:

- Nitrosomonas: bacteria that convert ammonia into nitrites.
- Nitrobacter: bacteria that convert nitrites into nitrates.

In an aquaponics system, the bacteria responsible for this process form a biofilm on all solid surfaces throughout the system that are in constant contact with the water. The biofilm – or "bio-filter" – can best be described as the odorless "slime" felt on all surfaces of the system and on the fish themselves. The submerged roots of the vegetables have a large cumulative surface area; so many bacteria can accumulate there. This surface area, together with the concentrations of ammonia and nitrites in the water, determines the speed with which nitrification takes place. Care for these bacterial colonies is important to regulate the full assimilation of ammonia and nitrites. This is why most aquaponics systems include a bio-filtering unit, which helps facilitate growth of these microorganisms. Typically, after a system has stabilized, nitrate levels range from 2 to 150 ppm. During system start-up, spikes may occur in the levels of ammonia (possibly as high as pH 11.6, which is pure ammonia), and an introduction of an acidic – such as distilled white vinegar – may be required to move the pH level closer to the desired 7.0 start-up & operating level.

Operation of an aquaponics system involves the input of five main components: water, oxygen, light, fish food and electricity. Ideally, with proper conditions, the fish population will propagate itself, but to retain a stable system spawn, or fry, may be added to replace grown fish that are taken out for consumption.

The ten primary guiding principles for creating successful aquaponics systems have been issued by Dr. James Rakocy, director of the aquaponics research team at the University of the Virgin Islands, based on extensive research done as part of the Agricultural Experiment Station aquaculture program:

1. Use a feeding rate ratio for design calculations.
2. Keep feed input relatively constant.
3. Supplement with calcium, potassium and iron.
4. Ensure good aeration.
5. Remove solids.
6. Be careful with aggregates.
7. Use oversize pipes.
8. Use biological pest control.
9. Ensure adequate biofiltration.
10. Control pH.

Fish feed sources include fish meal derived from lower-value species. Ongoing depletion of wild fish stocks makes this practice unsustainable. Organic fish feeds may prove to be a viable alternative. Other alternatives include duckweed grown within the same aquaponics system that feeds the fish; excess worms grown from vermiculture composting, using prepared kitchen scraps; as well as black soldier fly larvae, prepared using composting grub growers.

Water usage does not typically involve discharging or exchanging water but instead recirculates and reuses water effectively and efficiently. The system relies on the relationship between the animals and the plants to maintain a stable aquatic environment that experiences a minimum of fluctuation in ambient nutrient and oxygen levels. Water is added only to replace water loss from absorption and transpiration by plants, evaporation into the air from surface water and removal of biomass such as settled solid wastes from the system. As a result, aquaponics uses approximately 2 percent of the water that a conventionally irrigated farm requires for the same vegetable production. This allows for aquaponic production of both crops and fish in areas where water and/or fertile land is scarce.

Electrical usage in aquaponic installations relies in varying degrees on human-produced energy, technological solutions and environmental control to achieve recirculation and water/ambient temperatures. However, if a system is designed with energy conservation in mind, using alternative energy and a reduced number of pumps by letting the water flow downward as much as possible, it can be highly energy efficient. While careful design can minimize the risk, aquaponics systems can have multiple "single points of failure" where problems such as an electrical failure or a pipe blockage can lead to a complete loss of fish stock.

### The *Aqua-Pod* and Hybrid Farm/Garden at CRA R&D

There are a number of distinct qualities of the *Aqua-Pod* and hybrid farm/garden:

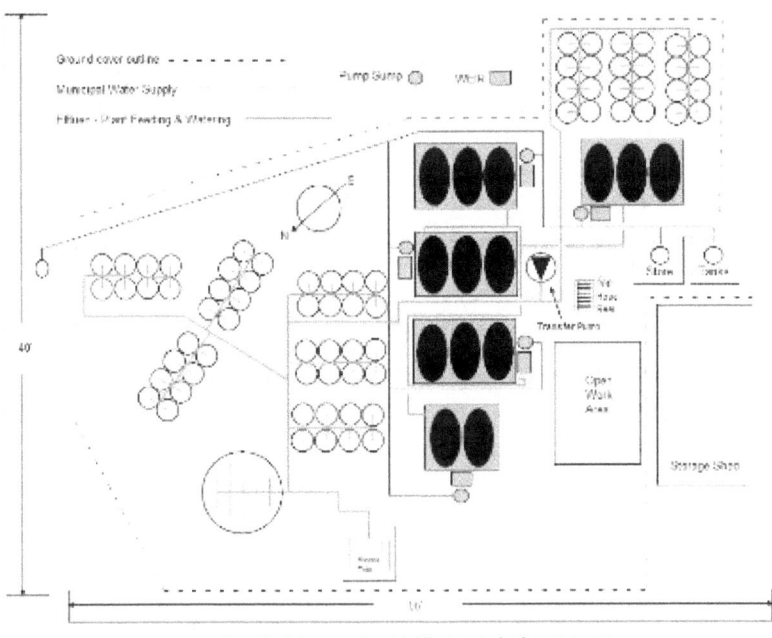

*The Farm at Cyrson Ranch Aquaponics R&D*

- The *Aqua-Pod* is a recirculating aquaponic system as discussed earlier. Specifically, the media base (several thousand high-fired pebbles) is installed in 216 four-inch net pots and effluent passes from one end of 12 ten-foot long grow tubes to the opposite end, where it is redistributed equally to three 150-gallon-tank/ponds. The media base provides a reservoir for strengthening the bio-filter with fluctuations in fish density and weight and plant density and size. The *Aqua-Pod* footprint is 52 feet square with a height of 7 feet.
- Platform components mirror those mentioned earlier, with the tank/ponds, sump, pump, gravity manifold and grow tubes. There is an additional "weir" tank located between the tank/ponds overflow and the unit sump to collect "heavies" (plant debris and such) and filter out pollywogs and snails.

- CRA R&D addresses the ten primary guiding principles for creating successful aquaponics systems in the following manner:

  1. Use a feeding rate ratio for design calculations. Fish are fed solid food once daily, and any uneaten food is drawn off the tank/pond surfaces after ten minutes. Fish are fed duckweed twice daily and worms cultivated on site.

  2. Keep feed input relatively constant. See item 1.

  3. Supplement with calcium, potassium and iron. This is done on a weekly basis, with the addition of potassium, calcium, iron and magnesium at the weir.

  4. Ensure good aeration. CRA R&D supplements oxygen with a small air pump and stone for each tank/pond.

  5. Remove solids. Solids are removed with the use of a weir tank and tight nylon mesh filter to remove, primarily, pollywogs and snails. Water clarity is checked daily, along with TDS (total dissolved solids) and pH.

  6. Be careful with aggregates. There are no aggregates involved in the operation of the *Aqua-Pod* - high-fired pellets notwithstanding.

  7. Use oversize pipes – All return piping is ¾ inch with no adverse effects.

  8. Use biological pest control. At CRA R&D, AzaMax is the only commercial pest control used. We use plants, reflective disks, helpful insects and animals such as lady bugs, praying mantises, spiders and frogs, and we remove large harmful pests by hand.

  9. Ensure adequate biofiltration. TDS, pH, water clarity and odor are noted on a daily basis to ensure a balanced bio-filter and address any out-of-parameter issues.

10. Control pH. pH has been corrected once – during the launch of the initial bio-filter in 2009. Adjustment of pH has never been required since.

*Tilapia at the Cryson Ranch, Tampa Florida*

- Tilapia are herbivores, and for the most part, the solid pellets that CRA R&D feeds the fish are a vegetarian source. The fish are also fed duckweed grown on site twice daily, and roots trimmed monthly from the net-pot plants grown in the systems.

- CRA R&D uses a mix of aquaponic and aquaponically fed hybrid soil-based beds to control system nitrate levels (bio-filter balance). These methods provide a much greater plant output with the ability to grow plants in both mediums. We are able to research the different returns offered and develop techniques to achieve the greatest returns in the least amount of space used. Soil-bed nutrition – nitrates – is derived from the aquaponic platforms as effluents are transferred to the beds during scheduled "change-outs." The on-site use of water is less than 6 percent of that used in Big Ag (industrialized) farming. Soil-beds are also supplemented and treated with composted waste and sterilized manures and treated with micro/macro nutrients through "soil injection" techniques currently researched on site.

- Electrical use can run as high as $39.41 (USD) per month during cold spells requiring tank/pond heaters all month. Under normal circumstances (no tank heating) monthly usage is $5.81 per month per *Aqua-Pod*. As mentioned previously an aquaponics operation can be compromised where multiple "single points of failure" may occur, including the loss of electrical power and pipe blockage. With the *Aqua-Pod* design this has been greatly minimized with a "fail-safe" design mitigating electro/mechanical losses due to the use of passive returns. The loss of pump power, a pipe obstruction or a situation in which the pump does not properly shut down will not affect the levels in the tank/ponds, which could otherwise result in the destruction of the aquaculture.

- Each *Aqua-Pod* operation provides 216 sockets fitting four-inch net pots, with the pots sitting in 1 ¼'' to 1 ½'' of effluent, and the moisture leaches up to feed the plant base and roots while providing ample oxygen for growth. Accompanying each *Aqua-Pod* installation are 12 (originally 8) aquaponically fed hybrid soil-based beds comprising a 37.6 square-foot growth area. Hybrid soil-based beds are fed nitrates from the *Aqua-Pod* effluent and – as with the *Aqua-Pod* – minerals are supplemented to enhance soil-based production. Sterilized soil has been the medium of choice at CRA R&D because there is no development of algae as is found using wools, sand and gravel as tested on site.

- Plants are removed on a monthly basis and the roots trimmed back to the net-pot base to provide accelerated growth rates and eliminating any "pooling" in the grow tubes.

- Effluent flow rates for the *Aqua-Pod* vary due to a float-driven supply pump. When the returns from the tanks/ponds reach a level in the pump sump, the pump motor energizes, flow commences and the nutrients are renewed until the sump level drops and the pump stops. The pump runs approximately 12 hours per day and the *Aqua-Pod* flow rate averages .72 liters per minute.

- Soil-based beds are fed using a transfer pump with the suction from each *Aqua-Pod*.

There are a number of recommended resources:

- Theaquaponicsource.com
- Backyardaquaponics.com
- Friendlyaquaponics.com
- Literature issued by the Southern Regional Aquaculture Center (SRAC)
- Literature issued by the North Central Regional Aquaculture Center (NCRAC)

The above suggestions are but a few of many possible sources of knowledge and information available. Some – many – sites and references offer items for sale, but it is not my intent to guide you to any site to make any purchase. The internet is a fascinating option to acquire information and knowledge but it's also the "wild west" with its fair share of fast talkers and scam artists. If you encounter a problem in your work with aquaponics chances are you aren't going to "buy" your way out of it. Become familiar with what's out there and use it when needed. Aquaponics, in the not-too-distant future, will be required to feed the world as weather change continues and as water, natural gas and petroleum products diminish. Unfortunately, we are behind in the acceptance and development of this very valuable source of vegetable and protein production. Journey into the aquaponics community and read what's there. With the aquaponics *Aqua-Pod* you will quickly gain knowledge and expertise. With that knowledge, contribute to the aquaponics community and assist in its acceptance and growth. Working with the aquaponics *Aqua-Pod* and related farm/garden is much bigger than the simple scope of having fish and vegetables to consume. It remains important that the information be distributed throughout the community and world.

CRA R&D has never purchased anything – including books – from an online aquaponics website. It's all there and it's all for the taking at no cost to developer/operator.

## Farm/Garden vs. Commercial Aquaponic Operations

Though the commercial viability of aquaponics remains, at this time, a topic of debate – as water becomes scarcer; as regulatory bodies enact and enforce laws to contain harmful industrial fertilizers, pesticides and herbicides; as fossil fuels become depleted and more expensive; and as communities commit to greater control of their food sourcing (and the related costs) – the CRA concept, and all aquaponic methods, will become commercially viable as demand increases.

Aquaponics is not currently the "sweetheart" of investment banking or venture capitalists. Creating food with fish poop isn't all that attractive to the uneducated – both those uneducated regarding aquaponics and those uneducated about the methods of production of their current food stream. At CRA R&D we are certain – let me repeat, we are certain – that aquaponic production will not only become viable but that it may be one of the most important social and technical innovations of the 21st Century. Cyrson Ranch Aquaponics Research and Development is committed to the belief and concept that aquaponics may offer the greatest opportunity to continue to feed the world in the not-too-distant future. In 2008, when CRA R&D entered into design and production, we assumed aquaponics would achieve a solid footing worldwide in 50 to 75 years. We now believe aquaponics will be a major component of vegetable and protein production in the next 15 to 25 years. It will depend on the weather and the rapidly increasing effects of global climate change and the decreasing availability of water and fossil fuels. It will also depend on whether we know the process and can deliver on it.

It is a major goal in the development of the *Aqua-Pod* and the related farm/garden to produce food in a small-scale manner that could be expanded into a large-scale operation as demand increases. Due to the nature of production, the *Aqua-Pod* operator is an aquatic expert, a produce farmer, a fish cutter and a chemist. The same applies to everyone employed in the aquaponic production. The commercial aquaponic owner/operator employs year round, and the employee works on the aquaponic site throughout the year. The *Aqua-Pod* uses a very small footprint, providing the maximum nutritional return in the minimum space. The waist-high grow tubes are easy to seed, maintain and harvest. The hybrid soil-based grow beds are, for the most part, pest free and are raised to a more manageable height than in-ground crops. Increased savings from radically decreased water and energy usage, the elimination of fertilizer costs and the increased revenues from production of both protein and vegetables make the *Aqua-Pod* system quite attractive. The units can be turned around quickly and the introduction and growth of high-demand/high-return crops can be accomplished rapidly. High production, low costs, loyal employees and flexibility make a properly designed and operated commercial aquaponics operation quite feasible with a generous chance to make an honest profit. It is due to this belief that CRA R&D continues to operate and research various options available for when aquaponics takes hold in the commercial sector and the world community as a whole.

We know that the methods currently used to mass produce foods, often of questionable quality, will no longer be sustainable in the not-too-distant future. But the exact future methods of aquaponics – and all food production – are yet to unfold. Suffice it to say those methods will be radically different from food production as we currently know it, and the foods we currently take for granted, particularly proteins, will be much changed. The mass production of beef for consumption will be radically reduced, as will that of most large industrially grown animals. Huge swaths of land cultivated and managed with copious amounts of water, huge quantities of petroleum-based fertilizers, pesticides and herbicides, and tended to by automated machines demanding diesel fuels will no longer exist. Even chemical hydroponics, using excessive amounts of petroleum-created plant foods will be unable to survive. Busing pickers north as the season advances will become a thing of the past as the mega-crops disappear and the luxury of all types of produce all year-round fades into history.

## IV. CRA R&D: Mission Statement and History

I've included this information, originally written in 2012 as a press release, into the beginning of the manual to give the reader a chance to understand what ideas and concepts provoked the initial concept and development of the *Aqua-Pod* – from prototype to finished product – and the related hybrid soil-bed farm/garden operation. The first four years were an intense period of trial and error; testing and research; compiling and crunching numbers and all of this had to be accomplished within the confining (and humbling) realities of dealing with the weather and the seasons - the time constraints of growing and harvesting plants - while ensuring the health of the system's bio-filter and the well-being of the aquatic life. Included also, the reader will discover those points that drove our research and development concerning industrial agriculture – "Big Ag" - and its effect on our food stream, water use and quality, pollution of the air and soil and its harm to native plants, birds, animals and insects.

I strongly urge the reader to carefully examine the contents of this section before going further into the manual. As you work further through this manual you will see that we did not pursue all the endeavors initially planned. Also you will see changes that we subsequently initiated and continue, as a research and development project, to make to better the quality and output of the *Aqua-Pod* and related soil-based hybrid gardens. It will greatly assist you in understanding the *"how's"* and *"why's"* the *Aqua-Pod* was developed, assembled and operated. This information provides a good, solid foundation to proceed in building your own *Aqua-Pod* and related hybrid soil-bed garden.

## 2008 – Cyrson Aquaponics Research and Development Mission Statement

*"Develop a stand-alone aquaponics system integrating food sources of fish and plants. Achieve the maximum nutritional value with the least footprint as applies to space requirements and environmental impact."*

### Development – Minimal Requirements

*- Commercially produced nitrogen fertilizers require the use 49 billion m³ of natural gas per year (two percent of the world's capacity). Enough energy to heat and supply electricity to 25.6 million homes in the US.*

*- Aquaponics use no commercial fertilizers!*

**Reliability** – to be achieved through initial construction and enhanced as required. Aquaponics is the husbandry of plants and fish, and unnecessary losses were considered intolerable during the development period. The system developed was required – with no failures permitted – to operate throughout the initial two-year research period.

**Simplicity** – to be achieved through the use of a minimum of moving parts and employing readily available "off-the-shelf" components. The system uses one pump and tank resistance heating to maintain minimum tank/ponds temperatures when required.

- Aquaponics use 2 percent of the water used in industrial agriculture Big Ag methods.

- The Cyrson Ranch – a mixed aquaponic and hybrid operation - uses just 6 percent of the water used in industrial Big Ag methods.

- Industrial agriculture methods use 40 liters of water to produce a kilo of tomatoes.

- A kilo of tomatoes grown at the Cyrson Ranch requires 2.4 liters of water.

**Durability** – achieved through high-quality construction and materials. It should be noted that some 40 percent of the initial construction costs are committed to insulation against thermal shock.

## 2010 - Principles of Operation

**Components and hydraulics** - 150-gallon tanks are situated 18"
below 4" irrigation tubes running in 10 feet lengths. Each unit has 12
irrigation tubes, with 3 ⅝" holes cut to accommodate 4" hydroponic
net pots and a clay-pebble growing medium – 216 pots total.
Each *Aqua-Pod* has a footprint of 52 square feet with a 7' height. A
passive system using a full-tank overflow provides a sump level
from which an automatic level-sensing pump pulls a suction and
transfers the pond water to an elevated supply manifold, where it is
evenly distributed by gravity through ½" flexible supply tubing and
introduced to the irrigation tubes. The gravitational movement of
water then travels from the supply end of the irrigation tubes, across
the plant roots and then – through ½" rigid return piping – back to
the fish tanks in a "raining" manner, providing a rich oxygen source.

**Filtering** - The bio-filter is developed and maintained as a nitrogen-
rich effluent and transferred to the base of the plant roots. The plants
draw sustenance from the effluent and thus provide filtering. The
bio-filter – the most important component of the system – is closely
observed through monitoring of pH, TDS (total dissolved solids) and
visual clarity. A bio-filter "reservoir" is created with the use of
several thousand high-fired pellets situated in the 4" net pots;
providing a strong and stable bio-filter regardless of fluctuating fish
populations and weights or plant quantities and size.

**Weir baffling**, a secondary filtering technique, is incorporated as a
step between the tank overflows and the pump sump. The weir baffle
provides an area for barley concentration (for bio-filter health) and
the use of a nylon mesh to prevent ingress of solids (e.g., snails and
pollywogs) that can affect the flow through the supply manifold
nozzles.

## Operations and Maintenance: System Monitoring

- pH levels are monitored closely. Initially during the development of a proper bio-filter, pH climbed into the upper 8's (caustic) and was corrected by the addition of white vinegar (a mild acid) to maintain a mid 7's level. Since the establishment of a proper bio-filter no additional buffering has been required. System pH remains between 7.0 and 7.6.

- TDS levels are monitored closely. In traditional fish farming methods, "change-outs" are drained to canals, streams and lakes. They contribute negatively in much the same manner as other fertilizer runoff. Though aquaponics negates these effects for the most part TDS levels can fluctuate and require correction. There are four methods to maintain proper TDS: increasing plant bed size (providing a greater root base); growing plant species that are more readily capable of taking up a greater quantity of nutrients; reducing the size and/or weight of the fish population; and, using "change-out" methods where the nutrient-rich effluent is used to fertilize traditional earth-planted systems. Our research is conducted using traditional soil planters, and TDS levels are maintained by feeding/watering these – "hybrid" - plant beds. This increases daily water usage from 2 percent to a bit less than 6 percent of that used in traditional industrial Big Ag farming – or an increase from 8.4 gallons to 25.2 gallons per *Aqua-Pod* per day. The feed/water used in the hybrid soil beds satisfy requirements for both nutrition and irrigation and greatly increases vegetable production.

*- 35.5 percent of every energy dollar required in direct and indirect industrial farming methods goes to the purchase of fertilizer and synthetic pesticides.*

**- *Aquaponics use no commercial fertilizers or synthetic pesticides.***

- Water consumption at less than 6 percent of system quantity is quite low when compared with traditional industrial Big Ag methods and remarkably less when nutritional values per square area are taken into account. Water is drawn solely from municipal supplies, and no water is used from ponds, streams or supplies that may have been contaminated with wastes from warm-blooded mammals. Water for usage in the system is stored in two 275-gallon storage containments and chemically treated with sodium thiosulfate to ensure the removal of chlorines and chloramines. Though agitation and aeration can remove added chlorines, they do not remove chloramines – both of which can be harmful to fish in high doses. Current practice in municipal water treatment is often to use chloramines without notification. Analysis comparing energy costs to properly aerate and costs using sodium thiosulfate reveals the second method to be more efficient.

- Fish are drawn from several varieties. Blue tilapia currently inhabit seven of the 14 tank/ponds, with African cichlids in one tank, and fancy and common goldfish in two tanks. Four tanks remain open to accommodate increased stocks due to breeding and the introduction of new species – particularly the introduction of fresh water prawns in research. Each tank is lined with a custom-manufactured net that can be drawn; and fish are observed, counted, sized and removed in this manner. An indoor laboratory uses 15 tanks where comparable populations of the fish in the system can be observed. This area also serves as fry havens and medical tanks as needed. Duckweed and beneficial algae are grown to supplement the fish diet, and aquatic plants provide shelter and spawning areas in the system tanks.

*We are exhausting and polluting our soil and water. Industrial agriculture uses 70 percent of the planet's fresh water. According to the EPA, US agriculture contributes to nearly 75 percent of all water-quality problems in the nation's rivers, lakes and streams.*

## 2012 - The Future

## Plant Development

*In relying on chemical "inputs", we have <u>un-learned</u> how to farm! We have destroyed our soils and all the good "things" within. "Dirt" is now void of the bacteria, fungi's and the micro and macro critters that permit our plants to nourish, aerate and naturally resist drought, disease and predators.*

Plants research remains our major focus at CRA R&D as we develop the best methods through the various planting cycles. The Tampa Bay region offers two growing seasons with distinct qualities and requirements. Following recommendations of the local agriculture extension office and tailoring our methods to meet aquaponic techniques, we continue to research and develop gardening methods for the greatest varieties and the best returns. Plants are grown using two methods – the aquaponic grow tubes and hybrid soil-based beds – and progress is directly compared. Analysis includes comparing growth rate, vegetable size and taste. Suitable plants are reproduced through seeds and cuttings, and the heartiest and best-tasting plants continue to be re-grown while new varieties are introduced as seed becomes available. In the deliberate absence of pesticides, we use beneficial insect predators and mechanical removal of invasive insects. Bee hives on the farm greatly enhance cross pollination. Each plant is trimmed and maintained to ensure good growth.

*The current food system is responsible for one third of global greenhouse gas emissions; it is also fully dependent on fossil fuels*

***both for transport and because industrial pesticides, herbicides and fertilizers are petro-chemically derived.***

*Aqua-Pod* plants are removed on a scheduled basis and the roots trimmed. Seed propagation includes the growth of species and plant lines that have been historically "forgotten" – to bring these plants back and reintroduce them. It is our belief that the loss of many strains has resulted in a deterioration of naturally healthy and hardy vegetation having much greater abilities to resist pests and drought conditions. We also believe this research will provide vegetables of greatly enhanced flavor and fiber.

With these facts and disciplines in mind it is our future goal to:

- Determine and implicate "cross-growing" techniques for which research will return concrete analysis of how – and when – aquaponic plant cultures can be transferred to traditional soil-bed growing methods to produce the greatest yield and the greatest returns in nutrition and taste.

44

- Working with soils and soil conditioning in an organic manner to scientifically understand specific qualities required by various plants and to implement actions to treat soils, rotate plant growing patterns and create organically balanced methods and techniques.

*When chemicals that are designed to kill are introduced into delicately balanced ecosystems, they can set damage in motion that reverberates through the food web for years.*
*- Honeybee populations are plummeting nationwide.*
*- Male frogs exposed to atrazine become females.*
*- Pesticides are implicated in dramatic bat die-offs.*

### Fish development

- The following year will require continued attention to stock growth due to the addition of two Aqua-Pods placed on line in May of 2012. Tilapia – our main fish source – are hearty breeders and it is anticipated they will double the stock within 12 months.
- With four 150-gallon tanks, we intend to introduce fresh water prawns into the culture to observe and research.

- We will conduct fish feed research to include the expanded production of naturally occurring aquatic plants and worm growth.

It remains the goal at Cyrson Ranch that there is no "power feeding" of fish or dense populations for the sake of high returns in fish quantities or weights. The methods most often employed in industrial food-fish farming techniques are cruel and disease fostering, and they potentially pose a hazard to the wild population if farm raised fish are released into local waters.

**Farm Development**

Cyrson Ranch Aquaponics Research & Development: Locating Farm Layout

- In addition to conducting the research outlined above, we will introduce industrially grown local plants into the culture to compare, and possibly compete, with industrial – Big Ag - methods. These will include several varieties of tomatoes along with bell peppers, snap beans, cucumbers, okra and squash.

- Ornamental flower development and growth remains a research issue in development for commercial application.
- We continue to promote the farming alternative of "on the farm all year," where farm employment encompasses all aspects of the farm culture – the care and harvesting of both fish and vegetation – thus radically changing the face of farming as we know it in the US. The farm employee stays with the farm for the full year, participating in all aspects of production, and hence lives in, and fully participates in all aspects of, the community on a permanent basis.

*- Pesticides affect the bee population in the US – 20 percent of bee colonies are destroyed by pesticides annually.*

*- An additional 15 percent are affected by herbicides applied to flowering plants.*

*- Bee colony collapse can be directly linked to pesticides through direct contact and the development of "super pests" (mites) that have become immune to synthetic pesticides.*

### Chronology - 2008 to 2012

- 12/08: Conceptual design of the first unit – "Pee Wee" – during the attacks on Gaza Strip residents by Israeli military forces is developed. This unit focuses on the basic issues addressed in the Cyrson Ranch Aquaponics R&D initial mission statement.

*"People need a food source close to home. They need a food source that doesn't require traveling through hostile checkpoints and navigating barriers or hazards such as mine*

*fields and battle zones. The food must be grown with a minimum amount of water where water is not always safely or readily available."*
*– Jim Gibson, CRA R&D Aqua-Pod Designer and Plant Manager 2008*

- 04/09: Pee Wee is placed into service in two 150-gallon tanks with common and fancy goldfish and 12 irrigation tubes accommodating 34 four-inch plants and 36 six-inch plants.
- 06/09: Bio-filter is established; Pee Wee unit is successfully cycling.

*Buying and eating organic is an important way to protect your family's health and to support sound farming close to home. For many, it is also – and in a deeper way – a matter of justice and environmental sustainability for future generations and people and places far away.*

- 11/09: Technical data recording is designed for two-year research period. The second unit design – "Rosa Parks" – is conceived; a two-year "research period" commences.
- 04/10: Rosa Parks is constructed and placed on line; African cichlids and blue tilapia are introduced into system; the *Aqua-Pod* is born; research data tracking is expanded.
- 06/10 – The "mechanical" plant is constructed, and hybrid soil-based, aquaponically fed plant growth is initiated; the mechanical plant permits fluid transfers throughout various systems and components, greatly reducing labor time and water loss

*"We have experienced success greater than initially anticipated. I am currently into the third seed generation of a number of plants. I continue to apply new methods to seeding and developing plants. Cross-growing – the technique of transferring plants from the aquaponics system to soil – is a growing challenge in managing the best return with the best flavor. Bio-filter maintenance is the basic and most important aspect of my research, yet I am impressed with the variety of fish and plants I am able to cultivate while maintaining proper filter parameters. My research continues to provide workable, healthy alternatives to the conventional methods we see in industrial farming today."*
– Pam Cyr, CRA R&D Plant and Aquaculture Research 2011

- 03/11: The third unit – "Big Boy" – is constructed and placed into service; tilapia and cichlid stocks are split, and hybrid soil-based growing beds are increased; the mechanical plant is expanded to accommodate growth.
- 11/11 – The two-year research period is completed; system(s) viability is confirmed and future development designed.
- 03/12 – Construction is initiated on fourth and fifth systems; hybrid soil-based beds are increased and the mechanical plant is expanded to accommodate growth.
- 05/12 – Fourth and fifth units are placed into service; tilapia and cichlid stocks are split.
- 08/12 – Hybrid soil-based beds expanded from eight units per *Aqua-Pod* to 12 beds per *Aqua-Pod*. Total units increased from 40 to 60 soil-beds.

*"This farming technique has the potential to radically alter the landscape of local and commercial farming as we know it, using less than 6 percent of the water compared to current industrial methods. The only items imported are the original seed, fish, fish food and a small amount of electricity. The food produced is fresh and wholesome with no adverse environmental impact. The point of our research and development is to return – to the farmer and community – increased independence from industrial seeds, fertilizers, herbicides and pesticides."*

*– Jim Gibson, CRA R&D Designer and Plant Manager 2012*

## V. Constructing The *Aqua-Pod*

### *Aqua-Pod Systems #4 and #5*

If you have not already read "The *Aqua-Pod* - Mission Statement and History of Development" I urge you to take the time to review the information. It provides a greater depth for understanding the *Aqua-Pod* – the reasoning, the discipline and the goals deemed necessary in the design. A the mission statement says - the *Aqua-Pod* design provides the highest nutritional return while using the smallest physical and environmental footprint as possible.

### *Nutritional Analysis of the Aqua-Pod*

*Assuming the nutritional calorific value of tilapia at 432 grams per pound (USDA) and at 80 percent usage per pound, the food energy per fully operating Aqua-Pod (discounting plants and vegetation values) at any one time is 77,760 calories. Total protein is 16,387 grams. At USDA recommended intake of 2000 calories per day, the unit provides 38.88 person-days of energy; and at 25 percent recommended daily intake of calories of protein (USDA), the unit offers 155.52 person-days. It should be noted that tilapia, at 7.7 grams fat/pound and 0 carbohydrates, can be consumed in greater percentages of protein (up to 50 percent), providing, in reality, 77.8 person-days per Aqua-Pod. Calorific values of vegetables and fruits are quite low, but other qualities are well known. Suffice it to say that consumption of the aquaponics Aqua-Pod plant and vegetation production provides healthy carbohydrates, vitamins, minerals, flavonoids, carotenoids and polyphenols.*

### Section Components

1.  Location lay-out of the *Aqua-Pod*
2.  Frame Construction
3.  Tank/Ponds Installation and Piping
4.  Grow Tube Modifications and Fluid Return Piping
5.  Gravity Supply Manifold Modification, Construction and Suspension
6.  Weir Tank Modification and Installation
7.  Sump and Sump Pump Installation
8.  Gravity Manifold Supply Piping
9.  Gravity Manifold Feeds to Grow Tubes
10. Electrical Considerations and Installation
11. Unit Top Covers
12. Tank/Ponds Apron/Skirts
13. Final Discussion – Common Sense and SAFETY!
14. Consolidated Materials and Costs List
15. Consolidated Tools List

## 1. Location and Layout of System

Locate the *Aqua-Pod* in full light. If sunlight needs to be tempered, it can be accomplished by growing light-sensitive vegetation among light-hardy plants for shade.

Location requires a flat surface. Place a good garden/greenhouse ground cover extending 32" past the basic footprint, and staple it securely to the soil. Place four 8" × 8" paving stones on the outer four corners where the structure will rest. When designing the CRA R&D project, we determined that taking the initial expense and time to install a good ground cover outweighed the labor and time that would be involved in keeping plant life around the *Aqua-Pods* trimmed back and manageable in the semi-tropical environment of the Tampa Bay, Florida, region. It is up to the potential operator to assess the local situation concerning ground cover installation. Interior operations – greenhouses or artificial lighting – may preclude the use of ground covering.

## 2. Frame Construction

The aquaponics *Aqua-Pod* is designed to provide the greatest nutritional value with the smallest footprint. The unit supports 12 grow tubes to accommodate 216 four-inch net pots. The three aquaculture tank/ponds are 150 gallons each, for a total of 450 gallons, with a potential yield of 225 pounds of fish at 0.5 pounds per gallon. The unit stands 7' high, 5' 2" wide and 10' 1" in length with surface area of 52 square feet.

### 2.1 Tools required

- Wood cutting saw
- 4 foot level
- Hammer or Phillips head screw driver

- Electric drill and 1/8" bit
- 25' foot tape measure
- Four clamps – 0" to 12"
- Six "C" clamps – 0" to 6"
- 6' step ladder
- Large square – 2' × 3'
- Two people

## 2.2 Optional tools

- Compound miter saw
- Table saw
- Drill press
- Power nailer (Paslode)

## 2.3 "Dimension" wood and specific cuts

*Concerning "pressure treated wood" - the USDA does not accept pressure-treated woods as usable with the production of "organic" vegetables. Being aware of this prior to development and construction, we determined the project would move forward with treated wood regardless of that limitation for the following reasons: 1) the treated wood has little to no contact with the vegetation; 2) it poses no hazard to aquatic life; 3) untreated wood in a tropical environment is impossible unless one wants to rebuild the units every several years; 4) our research needed to commence, and; 5) at CRA R&D it is our opinion the entire "organic" discussion has been "high-jacked" by corporations and industrial Big Ag, and most foods labeled "organic" may or may not be truly organic. True aquaponics, due to the very nature of raising and maintaining an aquaculture, must be organically wholesome. Fish do not tolerate chemicals, pesticides, herbicides and industrially produced fertilizers.*

**2.3.1** Four 2" x 6" x 8', cut to 7'2 ": *outside corner vertical supports*

**2.3.2** Four 2" x 4" x 8', cut to 7'2": *mated outside vertical corner cuts*

**2.3.3** Four 2" x 4" x 8', cut to 7'2 ": *vertical supports located between tanks/ponds*

**2.3.4** Two 2" x 6" x 10', no cut required: *horizontal length-top members*

**2.3.5** Two 2" x 4" x 10', no cut required: *horizontal length-base members*

**2.3.6** Two 2" x 4" x 6', cut to 59": *horizontal width-base members*

**2.3.7** Two 2" x 6" x 6', cut to 59": *horizontal width-top members*

**2.3.8** Four 2" x 4" x 6', cut to 59": two "scabbed" together for *end-unit grow-tube supports*

**2.3.9** Two 2" x 4" x 6', cut to 59": *mid-unit grow-tube supports*

**2.3.10** Two 2" x 2" x 10', no cut required: *support for system cover membranes and attachment*

**2.3.11** Two 2" x 8" x 8', cut to 16": *supply manifold supports*

**2.3.12** Two 2" x 4" x 8' cut to 59": *tank/pond top apron/skirt width supports*

**2.3.13** Two 2" x 4" x 10', no cut required: *tank/pond top apron/skirt length support as per above*

**2.3.14** Two 2" x 2" x 6', cut to 59": *return flow piping supports*

**Aqua-Pod Components Detail**

# 11 Not Pictured Here.

*2.3.1 through 2.3.14 - Aqua-Pod Components Detail*

To simplify the above requirements the following total cuts are required

- Four 2" × 6" – 10' cut to 7'2"
- Eight 2" × 4" – 8' cut to 7'2"
- Four 2" × 6" – 10'
- Two 2" × 6" – 10' cut to 59"
- One 2" × 6" – 10' cut to 59"
- Four 2" × 4" – 10' cut to 59"
- Two 2" × 2" – 10' (ripped 2" x 4" to 1 ½" × 1 ¾")
- Two 2" × 4" – 10'
- Two 2" × 8" – 8' cut to 16"

## 2.4 Additional requirements

- 2 ¼" galvanized "deck" screws
- 8d nails or power nailer (Paslode)

### Selecting wood for the *Aqua-Pod* construction

*Back before the advent of the "big box" store there were a number of privately owned yards where one could go and have a wood order filled or, at least, work with competent employees who would assist in the selection of wood to meet the needs of the project at hand. Those days have long passed and, though the prices paid at a box store seem lower, the reality is that the purchaser in on their own when selecting wood for this, and any, project.*

All of the pieces required for the construction of the *Aqua-Pod* are of; 2" x 4"; 2" x 6"; and, 2" x 8" dimensions and will all be of a #2 grade. Inspect each piece by "eying" the length. Reject any piece exhibiting a "bowing" or "sagging" action. Observe any knots, and try to stay away from any that might be "popping" and any piece with excessive knots along the edge of the wood. (knots are difficult to nail/screw through.) If the wood is gouged or otherwise damaged in manufacturing or transportation, put it aside. The 2" x 8" board needs two 16" lengths clear of knots. After checking the 2" x 8" piece as instructed above, scope out the two 16" "clear" (no knots) lengths that you will cut and modify for the supply manifold support. Save the receipts to return any wood (that hasn't been cut) for replacement.

*The wood doesn't have to perfect. There's only so much wood to be had in the world even as "sustainable" areas are re-grown. An experienced carpenter can use wood cuts that a novice finds difficult to work with, and will leave the best behind if not required. The Aqua-Pod – correctly constructed – will last 20(+) years. Pick materials you are confident in working with.*

## 2.5 Construction procedures

**2.5.1** Marry two of the 2 "x 4" mated outside vertical corner cuts (2.3.2) to two 2" × 6" outside corner vertical supports (2.3.1) to create an even-sided " EL" and clamp together. Nail or screw. If screwing, pre-drill. Remove clamps. Follow these steps and make an additional 3 EL supports to make up all four corners of the platform.

**2.5.2** With two of the corner supports laid on the ground, "C" clamp on the tank/pond top insulation width support (2.3.12) approximately 22 ½" from the bottom of the supports. Do not nail or screw.

**2.5.3** With the other two corner supports laid on ground, "C" clamp the remaining tank/pond top insulation width support

(2.3.12) approximately 22 ½" from the bottoms. Do not nail or screw;

**2.5.4** Place the two 2" × 4" × 10' horizontal length-base members (2.3.5) on surface between the corner pieces (2.3.1 and 2.3.2) and raise units, attaching them with the horizontal length-base members (2.3.5) and nail – or screw – once in the center of each to permit leveling the unit properly as it continues to be assembled.

It is suggested that a minimum of two people work as a construction crew, but during this stage four people are best. It can be done by one person, but it is difficult and time consuming.

**2.5.5** At approximately 22 ½" from the surface, "C" clamp the two 2" x 4" x 10' (2.3.13 to piece 2.3.2). Do not remove the clamps.

**2.5.6** Install the two 2" x 4" x 59" horizontal width-base members (2.3.6) and center nail/screw to the outside corner vertical posts (2.3.1) once in the center to permit movement when leveling platform.

**2.5.7** "C" Clamp the 2" x 6" x 10' horizontal length-top member (2.3.4) to the two top outer vertical corner supports (2.3.2) and level to the horizontal.

**2.5.8** Remove the clamps and tank/pond apron/skirt length supports (2.3.13).

**2.5.9** Check corner pieces for vertical plumb with a level; adjust with horizontal top member clamps and make adjustments with other clamped members – tank/pond top apron/skirt width supports (2.3.12). If necessary take a hammer and strike the corner pieces at the base and trim the clamped members if needed. Once the unit is vertically and horizontally leveled, nail/screw all components except the clamped component tank/pond apron/skirt width supports (2.3.12).

**2.5.10** Place all three tanks into the structure and set the tank/pond apron/skirt width supports (2.3.12) so they sit ½" below the tank lip and clamp. Do the same for the opposite end width (2.3.12).

**2.5.11** Clamp both tank/pond apron/skirt length supports (2.3.13) to meet/match tank/pond insulation width supports (2.3.12) and check horizontal leveling of both components and relationship to tank tops. When the unit true's with the level - vertically and horizontally - nail/screw components. Remove all clamps.

**2.5.12** Install horizontal width-top members (2.3.7) and clamp. True with a level and match location with horizontal length-top members (2.3.4). Nail/screw and remove clamps.

**2.5.13** The basic *Aqua-Pod* frame is now constructed. Carefully check all vertical and horizontal components with a level, and check with a large square for trueness. Use a hammer and "tap" components to meet the best requirements.

*This structure – constructed properly – can last 20(+) years. Take the time required to get it right. When you are satisfied, finish with ample nails/screws to secure the components well.*

**2.5.14** With the three 125-gallon tanks in the frame, mark where the four (two on each side) vertical supports between tanks components (2.3.3) should be placed – approximately 41" from the outside corner vertical supports (2.3.2). Remove tanks/ponds and attach these components after ensuring a true vertical plumb. Adequately nail/screw.

**2.5.15** Clamp the 2" x 4" x 59" end-unit grow-tube supports (2.3.8) 36" up, as measured from corner foundation blocks. Do not attach.

**2.5.16** Using two small blocks of 2" x 4", clamp at 36" up the closest vertical support (2.3.3) between tanks and set in one 2" x 4" x 59" mid-unit grow-tube support (2.3.9). Using the level, check for horizontal a true to end-unit tube support (2.3.8). Nail/screw component. Remove blocks and clamps.

**2.5.17** Using two small blocks of 2" x 4", clamp at 36" up the next vertical support between tanks (2.3.3) and set in one 2" x 4" x 59" second mid-unit grow-tube support (2.3.9). Using the level, check for a horizontal true to the previously installed mid-unit grow-tube support. Nail/screw the component. Remove blocks and clamps.

**2.5.18** Level check this component against the clamped end-unit grow-tube support (2.3.8) and adjust as needed. With horizontal relationships trued throughout length to grow-tube supports, screw both end-unit grow-tube supports (2.3.8) – do not use nails to attach these items. Remove clamps.

**2.5.19** Scab the 2" × 4"– 59" components to the inside of both end-unit growth supports (2.3.8) and screw. This provides adequate seating surface (four inches) for grow-tube support – do not use nails to attach these items.

**2.5.20** Take one 1" x 1 "x 10' support for system cover membranes (2.3.10) and attach – on one side – to the horizontal length-top member (2.3.4) ¾" from upper edge.

**2.5.21** Take the other 1" x 1" x 10' support for system cover membranes (2.3.10) and attach – on the opposite side – to the horizontal length-top member (2.3.4) flush with lower edge.

**2.5.22** The previous two steps provide a mounting surface – with a slight slope – for unit cover membranes and attachment of same.

# 3. Tank/Ponds Installation and Piping

## 3.1 Tools required

- Hacksaw and blade
- Tape measure
- Channel lock pliers

## 3.2 Optional Tools

- Electrical band saw

## 3.3 Materials required

**3.3.1** Three tanks/ponds: Rubbermaid 150-gallon Stock Tanks #4245 (livestock watering troughs). Selection and use of this tank is in keeping with the mission of "zero tolerance" of harm to the aquaculture. These units are indestructible, have an indefinite life span and have built-in piping components offering the highest integrity on the market. They can often be found available as "used" items at outlets such as Craig's List. It should be noted that there will be no after-market support for aquaponic systems constructed without the specific use of this tank.

*If the construction is being accomplished by a number of people, or over a period of time, use color-coded cleaners and glues. This reduces the chance that proper cleaning and gluing might be missed; resulting in joint failure. Particular care is required on any, and all, fittings below the upper lip of the fish tanks, as loss of integrity can result in tank-level drainage and death of the aquaculture.*

**3.3.2** Teflon tape for thread sealing

**3.3.3** Sandpaper for cleaning PVC pipe cuts

**3.3.4** Three 1 ¼" male NPT (National Pipe Thread) to 1 ¼" PVC sockets, schedule 40 straight adaptor

**3.3.5** Three 1 ¼" to ¾" reducing bushings. PVC male-socket to female-socket, schedule 40

**3.3.6** Three ¾" x 10' runs of PVC pipe, schedule 40

**3.3.7** Ten ¾" 90° PVC EL sockets, schedule 40

**3.3.8** Ten ¾" PVC TEE sockets, schedule 40

**3.3.9** PVC cleaner

**3.3.10** PVC glue

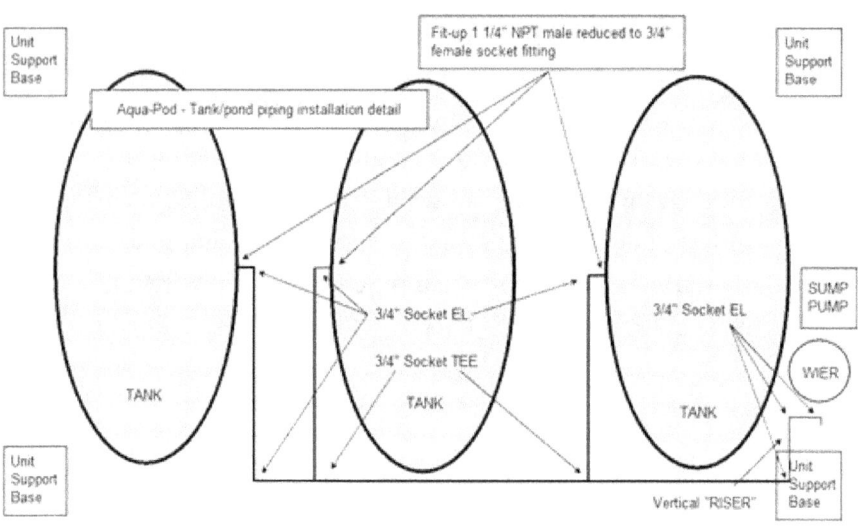

*Aqua-Pod Tank Piping Detail*

## 3.4 Installation of the tanks/ponds and related piping

*The Aqua-Pod is constructed in a fail-safe manner to eliminate, or maximally reduce, any possibility of a loss of water level in the tanks/ponds and the subsequent death of the fish. The following components are arranged and installed in the following manner so that, if there is a supply-pump failure, loss of pump capacity or over-pumping capacity; tank/pond levels will not be lost under any of these three circumstances.*

With tank/ponds outside of structure -

**3.4.1** Install three 1 ¼" NPT to 1 ¼" socket adapters (3.3.4) in tank/pond (3.3.1) using Teflon tape.

**3.4.2** Install three 1 ¼" to ¾" reducing bushings (3.3.5) by cleaning and gluing to each tank/pond.

**3.4.3** Cut three ¾" PVC pipe (3.3.6) lengths of 1 ½".

**3.4.4** Clean and glue one end of each cut pipe into a 3/4" reducing bushing (3.3.5).

**3.4.5** Line up tank/ponds in the manner they will be installed next to the *Aqua-Pod* frame. Two tank outlets – those furthest away from the collection point – will have outlets facing each other. The unit closet to the collection point will have its outlet facing away from the collection point (weir tank).

**3.4.6** Clean and glue ¾" ELs (3.3.7) so they are all going in the same direction and parallel to the ground surface.

**3.4.7** Install the tanks/ponds into the *Aqua-Pod* frame.

**3.4.8** Measure the distance from the tank/pond connection EL to the edge of the tank/pond, keeping inside of the *Aqua-Pod* lower frame, and cut three ¾" PVC pipes (3.3.6) to this length (24" to 26"). Clean and glue one end of the pipe to the EL coming off each tank/pond.

**3.4.9** On the tank/pond unit farthest from where the returns are to meet and be collected, clean and glue a ¾" EL parallel to the ground surface and in the direction of the collection point (weir tank).

**3.4.10** On the middle tank/pond and the closet tank/pond to the collection point (weir tank) glue two TEE's parallel to the ground surface.

**3.4.11** Between the end tank/pond EL and the middle tank/pond TEE cut ¾" PVC pipe to the required length (12" to 14"); clean and glue both ends, and install.

**3.4.12** Between the middle tank/pond TEE and the tank/pond TEE closest to the collection point (the weir), measure, clean and glue PVC pipe that you have cut to the required length (approximately 37").

**3.4.13** Measure, glue and install PVC piping (approximately 37") to terminate just inside of *Aqua-Pod* frame end (weir tank), and glue to the TEE. Don't "box" it in too tight.

**3.4.14** In the available space, install a ¾" EL horizontal to the ground and pointing back towards the center of the tank.

**3.4.15** Measure PVC pipe to run (6" to 8") from the EL installed in the previous step; clean and install.

**3.4.16** Install a ¾" EL perpendicular to the ground surface (pointing up) to accommodate the "vertical riser" installed in the following step.

**3.4.17** Measure and install the "vertical riser" so that it terminates just above/equal to the top of the tank/pond. Clean and glue and install lower joint of the riser to the EL installed in the previous step.

The height of the "vertical riser" (pipe length) determines the levels maintained in the tank/ponds for the *Aqua-Pod*. It is best to go a bit "long" on the cut of the "vertical riser" to permit adjustment (cutting) upon placing to unit into service. Ideally the levels of the tank/ponds should be ½" to 1" from tank/ponds "overflow" levels when in full operation.

**3.4.18** Where the riser terminates, place a ¾" EL facing away (outward) from the unit. Do not glue (see the above notes). Once the unit is placed in service, you will probably need to adjust the riser length to achieve optimum tank/ponds water levels.

**3.4.19** Cut a 3" to 4" length of PVC for flow to the weir tank and attach to previously installed EL. Do not glue.

**3.4.20** Attach the ¾" EL to the previously installed 3" to 4" length of PVC, facing down to direct flow to the weir tank. Do not glue.

Assembling the "overflow" components to the weir tank without gluing provides for both tank/ponds level adjustment and it permits the operator the ability to remove components to "back-blow" the lines occasionally.

**3.4.21** Fill the tank/pond to one third to one half level and check for any leakage and correct if necessary.

It's important for all fittings and pipes below the tank/ponds tops be tested to ensure construction integrity. The *Aqua-Pod* design is an inherently "fail-safe" in the sense that the tank/ponds can't be inadvertently "drained" due to a mechanical/electrical pump failure. But, if the pipes and fittings below the "water-line" are compromised levels can be drained and aquatic life lost

The following three sections require modifications to "off-the-shelf" materials. Particular attention has been made to detail these modifications. Prior to attempting any modifications, take the time to understand what is being modified and the reasons and actions involved. These components make the *Aqua-Pod* the productive and durable unit it is.

These detailed items can be farmed out into the community with an outreach plan. Schools, spiritual centers and community groups offer a wide range of talent and interests. Senior citizen housing often has a mechanical or carpentry club with a wealth of knowledge, skills and tools. Many high schools, community colleges and universities have shop classes that can assist while students earn credit for their work. Many churches, synagogues and mosques have clubs and members with the interest, tools and talent. Aquaponics is gaining interest in communities throughout the world. Reach out for help, and help will be there.

*Unit with properly installed tanks and piping*

# 4. Grow-Tube Modifications and Installation with Fluid Return Piping

*Twelve grow tubes are installed on each aquaponics Aqua-Pod providing 216 sockets for installation of net pots with high-fired clay pellets and plants. The grow-tube design, modifications and installation provide a strong durable, yet flexible, platform for growing a wide variety of plants and vegetation while ensuring a balanced and properly cycling bio-filter.*

## 4.1 Tools required

- Electric hand drill
- 3 ⅝" diameter hole saw
- 1 ¼" hole saw
- 45/64" drill
- 1/2" NPT tap
- 12" crescent wrench
- 12' tape measure
- Caulking gun
- Hack saw and blade
- Sandpaper or emery cloth – medium grit

***Working Grow-Tubes***

## 4.2 Tools recommended

- It is highly recommended that you use a drill press to make the sockets to accommodate the net pots. The increased power is helpful, but the primary value is the increased stability a drill press offers.
- A power band saw is an asset in this work as in many aspects of constructing components for the *Aqua-Pod* and farm/garden layout as a whole.

## 4.3 Materials

**4.3.1** Twelve runs of 4" x 10' schedule 20 PVC "drainage line" piping

**4.3.2** Twenty-four 4" PVC piping caps

**4.3.3** Twelve 90° ELs, ½" NPT to ½" socket

**4.3.4** Twelve 90° ELs, ½" socket to socket

**4.3.5** Eight 10' runs of ½" schedule 40 PVC pipe

**4.3.6** PVC cleaner

**4.3.7** PVC glue

**4.3.8** Teflon tape

**4.3.9** One tube of 3M Marine 5200 caulking

## 4.4 Grow-Tube Modification and Construction

The 10' tubes come with one end belled to be able to couple the tubes into a desired run. This is one reason these tubes were selected because, though it hasn't yet been done, the length of the *Aqua-Pod* can be doubled to 20' with six tank/ponds utilized. The current 10' construction requires the bell end be cut off with a hack saw just prior to the point where the bell begins to expand. Keep in mind that this end, like the opposite, will be capped. Test that the 4" caps fit, and, if required, remove another ½".

The grow tubes sockets are offset by 2" (staggered) from the tubes on either side. Thus six of the twelve tubes have their sockets offset 2" from the remaining six tubes.

*Grow-tube "Bell" detail*

*Cut the Tube "Bell"*

*Remove the Tube "Bell"*

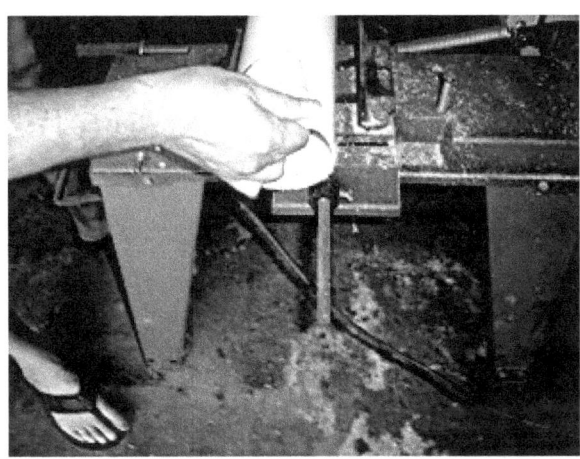

*Clean the Grow Tube after Cutting*

**4.4.1** Using the product labeling lines on each tube to maintain a straight line down each tube (use a straight edge to line blank areas in labeling if necessary) and make a mark 6" in from one end. This is the location of the first net-pot socket in the tube. Measure 6 ½" from this mark to locate the following mark and work down the length of tube marking at each 6 ½" interval.

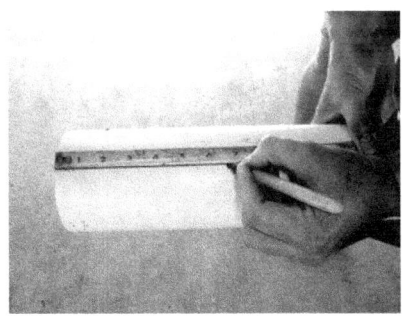

*4.4.1 Mark Grow tube "in" at 6 1/2 inches*

**4.4.2** After laying out the first tube, align it with 5 tubes (this can be done easily in the *Aqua-Pod* frame) and with a straight edge mark the positions for the 3 ⅝" socket holes on those tubes. Remove tubes and place to the side.

**4.4.3** Lay out the remaining six tubes and mark as follows: Come in 8" from the end and mark the first net-pot socket position. Mark each socket hole center 6 ½'' from the previous marking. Remove tubes.

*Grow Tubes Pot "Sockets" Staggered Properly*

**4.4.4** Using a drill or drill press with a 3 ⅝" hole saw, make holes at the points indicated during layout. A note of caution:

Be careful if using a hand drill as the hole-saw can bind; be prepared to release the trigger.

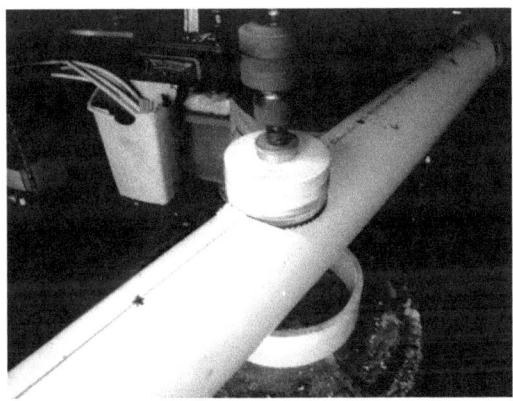

### *4.4.4 Cut Out 3 1/2 inch "Socket" Holes in Grow Tubes*

**4.4.5** Come in 3" from the ends of both tubes, where the initial 6" and 8" socket-hole measurement started, and mark. This is the hole through which the gravity line will feed nutrients from the gravity manifold to the grow tube. With a 1 ¼" hole-saw, make a hole in all 12 grow tubes.

### *4.4.5 Cut out 1 1/4 inch Holes in Grow Tubes for Gravity Feeds*

**4.4.6** Using abrasive sheets – sandpaper or emery cloth – clean the drilled holes of attached debris resulting from the drilling process.

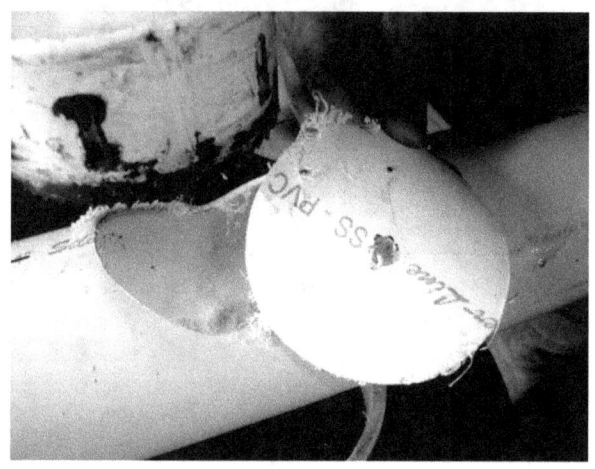

*4.4.6 Remove Cuts*

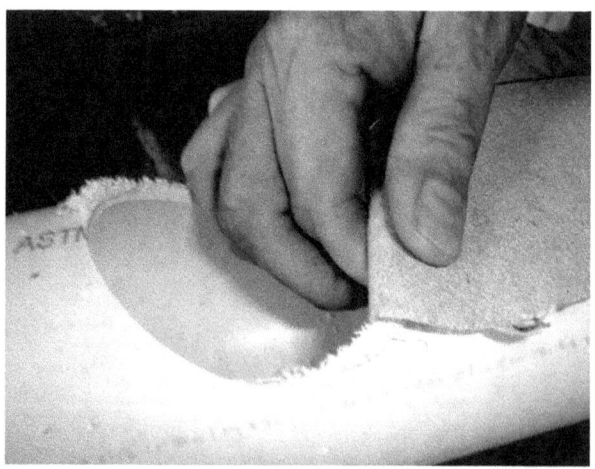

*4.4.6 Clean "Sockets" with a Sheet Abrasive*

*This might be a good time to throw something on the grill, make a large jug of lemonade and invite a few people by to help. There is enough of the unit put together to give people an idea of the Aqua-Pod is all about. Better yet – finish the next step of modifying and constructing the nutrient gravity manifold and then have a get together. Your visitors will be able to get a good look at the Aqua-Pod and the way it works and they can help with cleaning the tube sockets.*

**4.4.7** Attach a cap on the end where the nutrient feed hole is drilled by cleaning and PVC gluing. After gluing, place a thin bead of caulking between the tube and the cap, and smooth it with a water-wetted finger. Set to dry overnight. Repeat for remaining 11 tubes.

*4.4.7 Glue Caps to Grow Tubes*

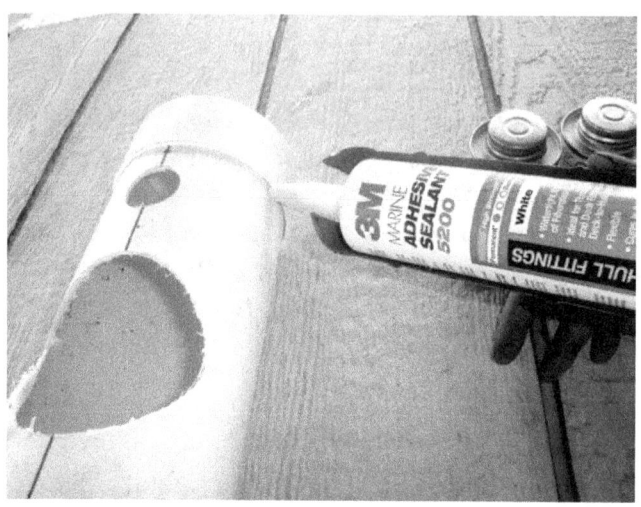

*4.4.7 Caulk Caps to Grow Tubes*

**4.4.8** With the remaining 12 caps, modify to permit the return flow to the tank/ponds by drilling a 45/64" hole in the center of each (2" from the circumference).

*4.4.8 Drill Cap for Return Flow*

**4.4.9** Using ½" NPT tap and 12" crescent wrench, "tap" the drilled hole. Run the tap down approximately ¾ of the tap thread length.

**4.4.10** On the opposite end of the grow tube, install the modified caps as described in 4.4.7.

**4.4.11** Place the tubes into the *Aqua-Pod* frame alternately to permit staggering of the socket pattern for better plant growth. Once installed, there will be 216 holes for placing four-inch netted pots.

**4.4.12** Teflon tape the threads and install 90° ½" NPT to socket fitting to tapped caps – female socket facing down.

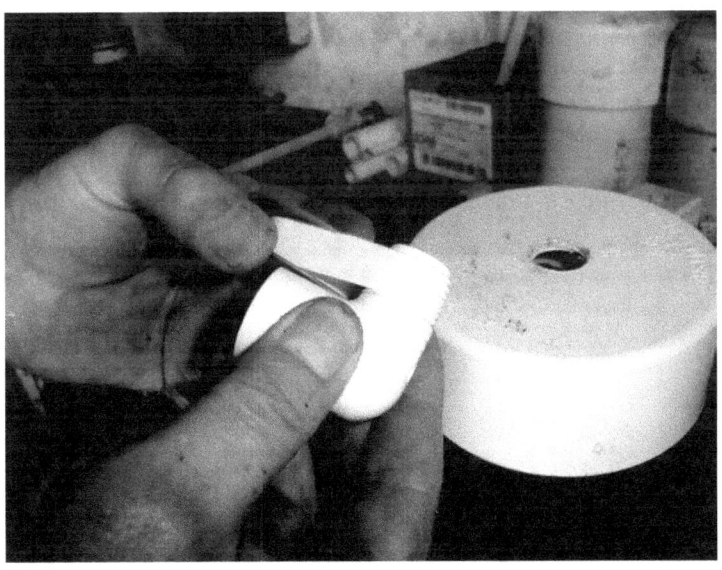

*4.4.12 Tape the 1/2 inch Fitting Threads*

**4.4.13** Cut twelve ½" pieces of PVC pipe at 5" lengths and install in sockets. Do not glue.

**4.4.14** Place twelve 90° EL's, ½" socket to socket facing back toward the tank/ponds. Do not glue.

*4.4.14 Example - Return Cap Installation*

**4.4.15** Cut ½" PVC pipe at appropriate lengths to feed back to the tanks/ponds – four return pipes per tank/pond. The lengths will be four each of at 18", 48" and 72". Rest the two longer lengths on the return flow piping supports as discussed in 2.3.14. Do not glue any of these components.

## 5. Gravity Manifold Supply Modification, Construction and Suspension

*Gravity Manifold Detail*

*The gravity manifold is the high point of the unit and provides distribution to each of the 12 grow tubes where the nutrients are taken up by the plants in net pots placed in the 216 sockets. It receives its supply from the system pump located in the system sump.*

The function of this component of the *Aqua-Pod* is to collect fluid nutrients at a high spot in the system to distribute, by gravity, to the 12 grow tubes and the 216 plant sockets contained within. As with the modification and construction of the grow tubes, attention to detail and concise modifications will provide a productive and durable component of the unit.

## 5.1 Tools required

- Hacksaw
- Electric drill
- 45/64" drill bit
- ½" NPT tap
- 12" crescent wrench
- Level

## 5.2 Tools recommended

- Power hacksaw
- Drill press

## 5.3 Materials:

**5.3.1** One PVC Pipe schedule 40 – 4" x 5' cut to 44"
**5.3.2** Two PVC Pipe Caps schedule 40 – 4" diameter
**5.3.3** Twelve ½" male NPT to ½" barbed fittings
**5.3.4** 1 – 90° EL, ½" male NPT to ½" barbed fitting
**5.3.5** Teflon tape
**5.3.6** PVC cleaner
**5.3.7** PVC glue
**5.3.8** 3M Marine 5200 caulking

## 5.4 Gravity manifold modification and construction

**5.4.1** Cut 4" schedule 40 PVC pipe to 44" length

*5.4.1 Cut the Gravity Manifold Tube to a 44 inch Length*

**5.4.2** Measure off one end at 6" and mark, for the center of the first ½" fitting.

*5.4.2 Measure and Mark Gravity Manifold Tube at 6 Inches*

**5.4.3** Continue down, in a straight line, marking at 3" intervals for 11 more points for fitting the 1/2" grow-tube distribution lines.

*5.4.3 Gravity Manifold Marked at 3 Inch Intervals*

**5.4.4** At 90 degrees off the 6th marked point mark for drilling and tapping. This is where the pump discharge enters to supply the distribution lines.

*5.4.4 Gravity Manifold Marked for Supply Line*

**5.4.5** The manifold is now laid out where the pump will discharge nutrients to the side of the manifold and flow to the tube exits through the bottom of the manifold.

**5.4.6** Using a 45/64" drill bit – drill thirteen holes as marked, paying attention to remaining true (i.e., do not "wallow out" the holes) to the 45/64" diameter for precise tapping results.

*5.4.6 Drill 12 Holes Marked at 3 Inch Intervals for Grow Tube Supplies*

*5.4.6 Drill Gravity Manifold for Sump Pump Supply*

**5.4.7** Tap all thirteen holes with ½" NPT tap to three quarters of the length of the tap thread surface.

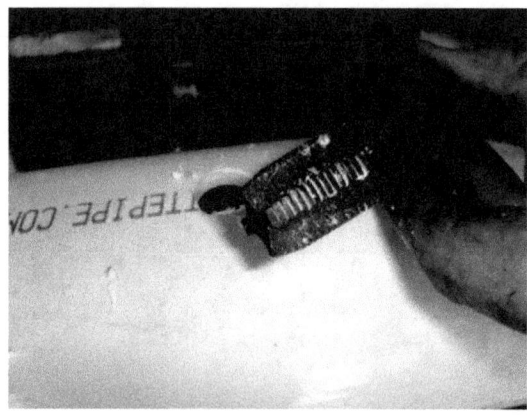

*5.4.7 Tap 13 Holes Drilled in the Gravity Manifold*

**5.4.8** Teflon tape the threads of twelve male ½" NPTs to the ½" barbed fittings, and install with the 12" crescent wrench.

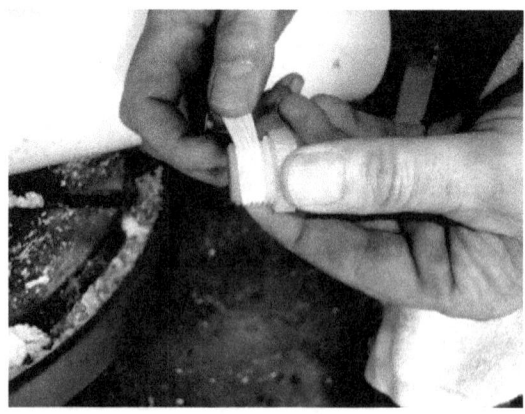

*5.4.8 Grow Tube Supply Fittings Taped*

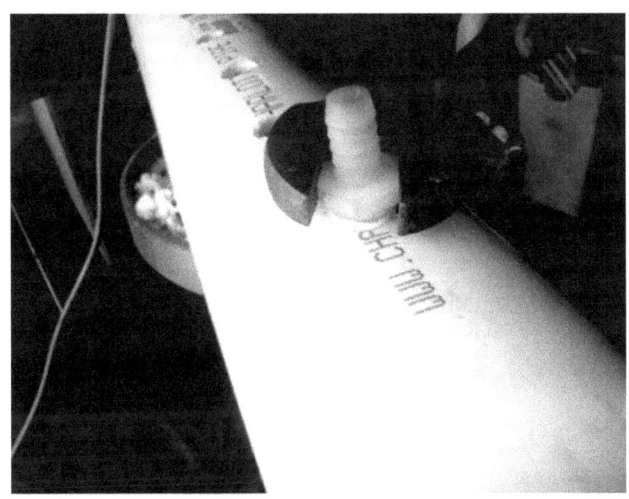

*5.4.8 Grow Tube Supply Fittings Installed*

**5.4.9** Teflon tape the threads of the 90° EL, ½" NPT to ½" barb – and install.

*5.4.9 Pump Supply Fitting Taped*

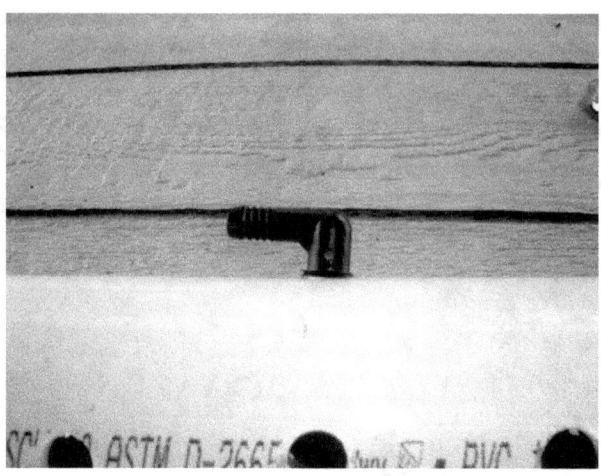

*5.4.9 Pump Supply Fitting Installed*

**5.4.10** Clean pipe ends with PVC cleaner and glue on the 4" diameter caps.

*5.4.10 Clean and Glue Gravity Manifold Caps*

**5.4.11** Caulk the end caps to ensure against leakage.

*5.4.11 Caulk Gravity Manifold Caps*

## 5.5 Gravity distribution header supports

*The gravity distribution manifold requires the use of two "clear" sections of 2" × 8" wood 16" in length. A "clear" cut of wood – also known as a #1 grade – has no knots or imperfections and can be quite expensive. The shortest length of 2" x 8" available is 10 feet, and with proper inspection and "picking", two satisfactory 16" "clear" runs can be had from a #2 graded stack of 2" x 8"s and will save the costs of a #1 grade purchase.*

## 5.6 Tools required

- Reciprocating saw – hand-held with 3" wood scrolling blade
- Straight edge
- Electric drill with Phillips head screwing bit
- 1/8" drill bit
- 5" hole saw
- 3' carpenter level

## 5.7 Tools recommended

- Drill press.

## 5.8 Materials required

- Two 2" × 8" cut to 16" "clear" lengths
- 2 ¼" galvanized utility screws

## 5.9 Gravity Distribution Header Supports ("Saddles") - Construction and Installation

**5.9.1** Cut two 16" lengths of "clear" 2" x 8 " pressure-treated dimension lumber.

**5.9.2** Measure and scribe a line 3" from the width (7 ¼ ") side end (following a kiln drying process "dimension lumber" - 2" x 8" is actually 1 ½" by 7 ¼").

**5.9.3** On the length (16") side come in 1 ½" and scribe the full length.

*5.9.2 and 5.9.3 Saddles Properly Scribed for Cuts*

**5.9.4** Position the 5" hole saw to cut inside of the 1 ½" line and inside of the 3" line. Take care in positioning. Remove the 5" round with the hole-saw.

*5.9.4 Cut the Saddle Hole*

*5.9.4 Remove the Saddle Hole*

**5.9.5** Using the power jig saw, cut from the inside of the hole, following the scribed 1 ½" line to the end of the piece.

*5.9.5 Cut the Saddle with a Jig-saw*

**5.9.6** At mid-circumference, on the opposite side of the hole, make a short cut and remove the cut piece.

*5.9.6 Cut the Saddle again with a Jig-saw*

**5.9.7** On the bottom corners cut two 45° angles to stress relieve the members and ensure long-term integrity.

*5.9.7 Cut 45 degree Angles off Bottom Corners*

**5.9.8** Lightly sand the all edges of the distribution manifold supports.

***5.9.8 Saddles Sanded and Ready to Install***

**5.9.9** Clamp the gravity distribution manifold supports onto the horizontal width-top member (2.3.7) on the side of the unit where the weir and sump tanks are located. Set the manifold in place and adjust both hangers for proper positioning between nozzle tube fittings.

**5.9.10** Place a level on top of the manifold and true to horizontal.

**5.9.11** Drill with 1/8" drill bit and then secure with two 2 ¼" screws per hanger.

**5.9.12** Cut the excess from the top of the unit with a handsaw or power jig saw.

*Saddle Installation Detail*

*These detailed items can be farmed out into the community with an outreach plan. Schools, spiritual centers and community groups offer a wide range of talent and interests. Senior citizen housing often has a mechanical or carpentry club with a wealth of knowledge, skills and tools. Many high schools, community colleges and universities have shop classes that can assist while students earn credit for their work. Many churches, synagogues and mosques have clubs and members with the interest, tools and talent. Aquaponics is gaining interest in communities throughout the world. Reach out for help, and help will be there.*

## 6. Weir Tank Modification and Installation

The weir tank functions as a collection point for returns from the tank/ponds and provides a place for simple filtration of the *Aqua-Pod*. The first method of filtration is gravity, where "heavy's" settle to the bottom of the weir and are periodically drained into the hybrid soil-based plants. The second method is a nylon "knee high" tied to the return line into the weir tank. This method is primarily to filter out snails and pollywogs that get into the system that, if permitted into the sump bucket, will clog the distribution nozzles to the grow tubes. Periodically these are renewed. Used nylons are dried and sliced open and the nutrient-rich contents added to the composter(s).

## 6.1 Tools required

- ¾" drill bit. A "power bore" bit works best because of its leading edge with a cutter. Go slow and let the leading edge do its job. Since the thickness being drilled/cut-out is small, the leading edge will do all the work. Other ¾" bits can be used carefully. Do not wallow out the hole. The perfect job will require the male coupling to be gently screwed into the weir bucket upon installation. Cut the hole in the weir bucket 2 ½" from the top on the width face.
- Hack saw to cut one piece of ½" schedule 40 PVC pipe.

## 6.2 Materials required

- One 5-gallon weir bucket. An inexpensive trash can (waste basket) has been used because it offers a flat area to install the overflow piping with the least chance of leakage. History has proven that installations in round "utility" buckets (a 5-gallon "spackle bucket") can lead to leakage. These "waste basket" units have proven effective for 5(+) years with no issues.
- One ½" EL socket
- One 4" run of ½" PVC pipe – schedule 40
- One ½" coupling socket on one side, and ½" threaded NPT (female) on the other side
- One ½" male NPT to female socket fitting

- One "O" ring that goes over the threads of the preceding item. This is the water seal; it was arrived at by taking the component and eye-balling "O" rings at the faucet area of the same "box" store where the other materials were purchased. Fortunately it worked the first time and these are the dimensions: outside diameter = 1 3/32", inside diameter = 29/32", "O" Ring thickness = 1/8". The exact dimensions aren't critical. Bear in mind the function required and go from there. If needed, take the components to the local auto supply store, describe the function and have them size it with you.

## 6.3 Weir Tank Assembly

**6.3.1** Drill a 1/2" hole on the "trash-bin" narrow with approximately 2 1/2 inches from the upper lip.

**6.3.2** Place an "O" ring over the male threads of the 1/2" male NPT to female socket fitting.

**6.3.3** Insert the male fitting from the inside of the trash bin through to the outside.

**6.3.4** Screw the 1/2" female NPT coupling onto the male threads emanating from the trash-bin and "squeeze" up on the connection to engage the "O" ring to create a water tight seal.

**6.3.5** Install the 4" run of tube from the female socket with the 90 degree 1/2" EL pointing down.

**6.3.6** Once assembled, place the weir under the tank/ponds overflow to catch the returns.

**6.3.7** Place three 12" x 12" pavers under the weir to raise it to the appropriate height for the proper gravity overflow to the pump sump. These fittings do not have to be glued.

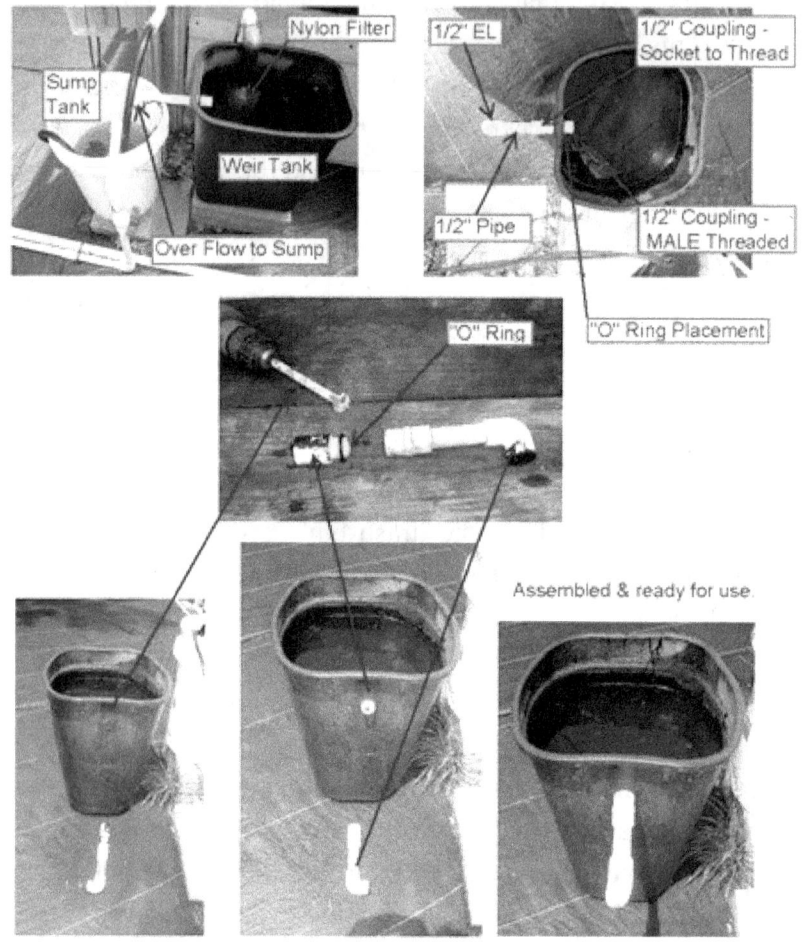

WEIR TANK DETAIL

*The comforting aspect of the weir tank and all involved components is that it is on the "high" side of the system, meaning if any component fails it will not drain the tank/ponds, and no loss of aquatic life can occur. There has never been a problem with this arrangement on any of the five weir tanks installed at CRA R&D.*

# 7. Sump and Pump Installation

The sump receives its supply as the weir tank overflows. At a sufficient level in the sump, as sensed by a level switch, the submerged sump pump energizes to deliver effluent to the gravity supply manifold, which in turn supplies the grow tubes. As mentioned earlier, the weir tank is elevated above the pump sump but low enough to catch the tanks/ponds overflows.

## 7.1 Tools required

- Diagonal wire cutters
- Straight shank (blade) screwdriver

## 7.2 Materials required

**7.2.1** Submersible pump – 205 GPH, 110V, 70 Watts

**7.2.2** Sump "series" operating float

**7.2.3** 5-gallon utility bucket

**7.2.4** EL fitting – ½" Female NPT to ½" barb

**7.2.5** Short electrical wire wraps

**7.2.6** 3' length of ½" flexible PVC hose

**7.2.7** ⅜" to ⅞" hose clamps

*The vast majority of the mechanical items used are manufactured outside of the USA, and what was used initially may not be available in the future. For example, the ½" flexible PVC hose used in the construction of the first three Aqua-Pods assembled at CRA R&D was unobtainable in the construction of the final two Aqua-Pods. Hence we were required to use ⅜" to ⅞" hose clamps to reliably secure tubing onto the barb fittings.*

## 7.3 Sump pump installation instructions

*7.3 Sump Detail with Submerged Pump and Float Switch*

**7.3.1** Tape the ½" pump discharge threads with Teflon tape.
**7.3.2** Install the 90° ½" female NPT to ½" barb fitting, with the barb pointing up from the bottom of the pump.
**7.3.3** Using a utility knife, cut and attach the 3' length of ½" flexible PVC to barb fitting and, if necessary, secure with a hose clamp using a screwdriver.
**7.3.4** Place the pump sump bucket under the weir tank overflow.
**7.3.5** Place the float switch in with sump pump and use wire ties to loosely secure the float cord to the pump electrical supply cord. Positioning of the float switch will require "tweaking" the position of the wire wraps when the unit is placed into service. Cut excess tie wrap lengths.

**7.3.6** Plug the float into a ground fault interrupting (GFI) electrical supply outlet.

**7.3.7** Plug the pump electrical supply into the float switch outlet.

**7.3.8** The 3' length of ½" flexible PVC is to be sized for a final cut as discussed in the following section (8.3.10).

## 8. Gravity Manifold Supply Piping Installation

The sump pump discharge must be routed to the gravity manifold. The method described here offers an inexpensive and durable method of installation.

## 8.1 Tools required

- 9/16" auger bit
- Hacksaw
- 12" measuring tape
- Phillips head screwdriver
- Utility knife

## 8.2 Materials required

**8.2.1** One 5' length of ½" PVC pipe schedule 20

**8.2.2** One 5' length of ½" flexible PVC

**8.2.3** Two ½" couplings female socket to female NPT

**8.2.4** Two EL's, ½" male NPT to ½" barb fittings

**8.2.5** Two ⅜" to ⅞" hose clamps

**8.2.6** Two 9/16" "U" pipe straps

**8.2.7** Four 1" utility screws

## 8.3 Installation of gravity manifold supply piping

**8.3.1** With gravity manifold placed into the saddles, use the 9/16" auger bit to drill a hole in the mated outside vertical corner (2.3.2) level with gravity manifold inlet fitting.

**8.3.2** Glue the ½" socket to female NPT coupling to the top of the 5' length of ½" PVC pipe.

**8.3.3** On the ½" 90° EL male NPT to barb fitting, Teflon tape the threads, and screw into top of pipe with the coupling installed as per the preceding step.

**8.3.4** On the barb fitting attach ½" flexible PVC and secure with hose clamp if necessary.

**8.3.5** With pipe in place at upper end, mark the lower end approximately 8" above the top of the sump bucket.

**8.3.6** Remove the pipe and cut at the mark as indicted.

**8.3.7** Replace the pipe into service and size the upper ½" flexible tubing to reach the gravity manifold supply fitting barb and cut with a utility knife. Attach it to the barb fitting on the gravity manifold and secure with a hose clamp if necessary.

**8.3.8** At the pipe bottom, glue the ½" socket to female NPT coupling to the re-sized (8.3.5) 5' length of ½" PVC pipe.

**8.3.9** Teflon tape male threads of ½" 90° EL male NPT to ½" barb and tighten into place, with the barb fitting extending away from the *Aqua-Pod* frame over the sump bucket.

**8.3.10** Size, cut and attach pump discharge hose (7.2.8 above), and secure with a hose clamp if necessary.

**8.3.11** Secure the pipe to the frame using 9/16" – "U" pipe straps.

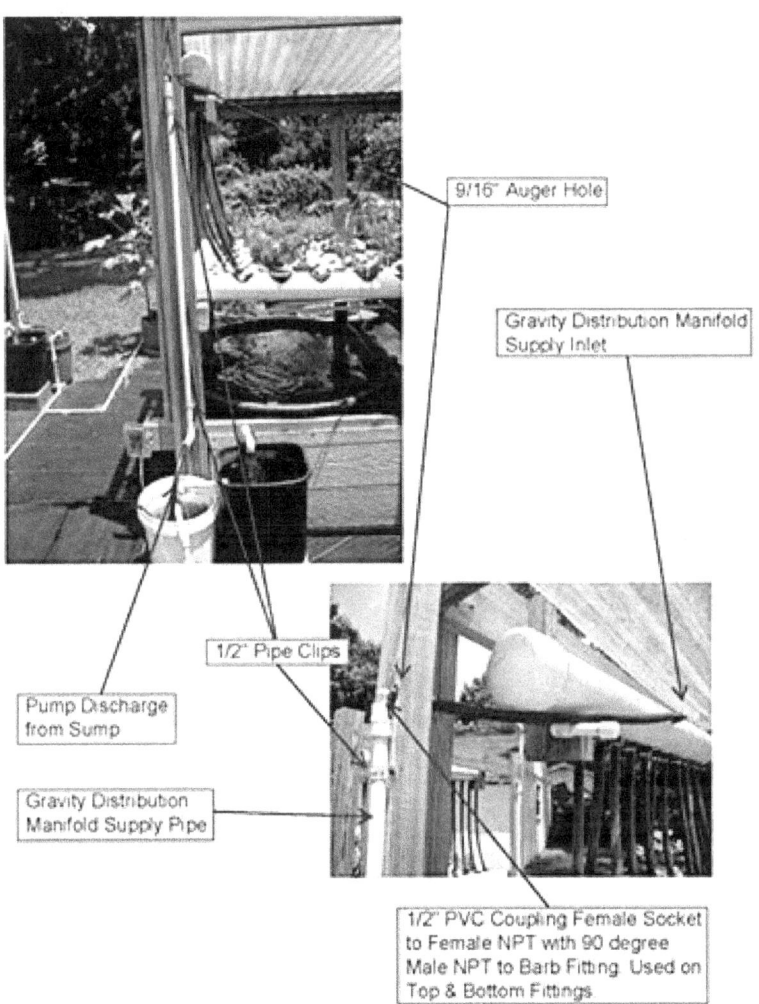

9/16" Auger Hole

Gravity Distribution Manifold Supply Inlet

1/2" Pipe Clips

Pump Discharge from Sump

Gravity Distribution Manifold Supply Pipe

1/2" PVC Coupling Female Socket to Female NPT with 90 degree Male NPT to Barb Fitting Used on Top & Bottom Fittings

Pump Supply to Gravity Distribution Manifold

## 9. Gravity Manifold Feeds to Grow Tubes Installation

The gravity manifold is "charged" with the sump pump discharge and distributes, by gravity, effluent feed to each of the 12 grow tubes, which in turn feed effluent to the plants in net pots placed in grow tube sockets.

### 9.1 Tools required

- 12" tape measure
- Electric drill
- 1/8" drill bit
- Straight shank (blade) screwdriver
- Utility knife

### 9.2 Materials required

- One 30' length of ½" flexible PVC tubing (sprinkler tubing)
- Twelve ½" straight NPT to ½" barb fittings
- Twelve ½" NPT threaded caps with 1/8" hole drilled in cap center
- Twenty-four ⅜" to ⅞" hose clamps

*As mentioned earlier, many of the mechanical items used in the Aqua-Pod construction are manufactured outside of the USA, and product specifications often change. You may find a need to use hose clamps to properly secure the barb fittings.*

*9.3 Gravity Manifold Feeds to Grow Tubes Detail*

## 9.3 Installation instructions

**9.3.1** Using the electric drill and 1/8" drill bit, make a centered hole in each of twelve ½" PVC caps.

**9.3.2** With the gravity manifold in place, measure, with flexible measuring tape, from the top of the barb fitting on the gravity manifold to just above the ¾" feed hole on the first grow tube. Cut a length of ½" flexible PVC as measured.

**9.3.3** Install the flexible ½" PVC to the barb on the gravity manifold.

**9.3.4** Place the ½" barb at the lower end of flexible ½" PVC hose and loosely screw the ½" NPT cap into place.

**9.3.5** Check for proper length with the cap fitting into the ¾" hole approximately half of the cap's ¾" length. A proper fit provides the freedom to remove it without a possibility that the line will become free during operations, resulting in the loss of feed/water. Make any length adjustments necessary and use hose clamps if required.

**9.3.6** Repeat the preceding steps for the remaining eleven grow tube feed/watering lines.

## 10. Electrical Installations and Considerations

*Any and all electrical supplies must be ground-fault interrupted (GFI) and be within local/national code requirements. When in doubt, consult a licensed professional in all matters concerning electrical installation and use.*

Two components of the *Aqua-Pod* require electricity full-time – the pump (runs intermittently) and three small air pumps (40-gallon aquarium units). In addition, three 400-watt tank heaters draw electricity part-time if the tank/ponds temperature drops below 65°F. Air pumps are installed to supplement the primary oxygen developed by the gravitational drop of water returning from the grow tubes. The five *Aqua-Pods* installed at CRA R&D have run their electrical supplies overhead off of a central 200-amp service; they are installed to code and protected with 15-amp breakers. As your installation may not reflect the conditions at CRA R&D, there are a number of considerations to take into account. A solo unit may be able to be run simply through an extension cord. Interior units (greenhouse and grow lights) can be powered through overhead runs of cord/wire. With pump selection modifications (Direct Current) and/or the use of a power inverter, an *Aqua-Pod* can operate off wind and solar voltaic production. For this reason, discussion concerning electrical supply is limited.

*Aquaponics – any and all types – is a wet business. Read, and heed, this warning!*

## 11. *Aqua-Pod* Top Cover Membranes

The units are top covered for several reasons. The sun in the Tampa Bay region can be brutal, and the covers used – reducing light transmission by 7 percent – make life a little easier in the summer months, particularly relating to seedlings. Covers also greatly reduce the introduction of (acid) rain to the tank/ponds and assist in preventing bugs from getting into the vegetation. Birds don't appreciate the covers and, for the most part, stay out of the systems. If the weather gets too cold, the units can "wrapped" in clear food wrap and, with the top covers in place and the water heated, a cold spell can be toughed out.

## 11.1 Tools required

- Aviation shears
- Gloves
- Straight edge
- Tape measure
- Phillips head screwdriver

## 11.2 Materials required

- Fourteen #8 ½" lathe screws
- Two 12' × 26" corrugated roofing panels – clear (Tuflex – UltraVinyl)
- One 8' × 26" corrugated roofing panel – clear (Tuflex – UltraVinyl)

## 11.3 Preparation and installation of unit top covers

*11.3 Top Membrane Detail*

**11.3.1** Measure the distance between cover membrane supports (2.3.10) for precise cut lengths – approximately 57".

**11.3.2** Scribe the required length on the roof panel and cut with shears: four cuts out of the two 12' panels and one cut out of the 8' panel.

**11.3.3** Install the panels overlapping by at least 2" on each side. Due to excess some overlapping will exceed 2". There will be an opening of 1 ½" at one end due to the installation of the gravity manifold support saddles. This isn't an issue as the cover doesn't have to be totally tight.

**11.3.4** Where the panels overlap install a lathe screw and install a lathe screw at the four corners.

*11.3 Top Membrane Detail*

***The selection of corrugated roofing panel should primarily be based upon cost and durability. The Tuflex is a 3-mil UV-protected design, and it has proven durable; no repairs or replacements have been required. The Tampa Bay region can be quite windy with strong UV rays, but we have had no issues concerning failure of this type of panel.***

## 12. Tank/Pond Apron/Skirt

The units in the Tampa Bay region have skirting installed from the ground surface to just below the upper edge of the fish tanks. This is done for two reasons: thermal protection and esthetics. The tank/ponds are skirted to reduce the effects of wind shear while providing an air insulation barrier between the ambient atmosphere and tank/ponds. During the first 24 months of operation a large number of variables were measured, and one of the greatest differences discovered was the temperatures, and the rate of temperature change, of the skirted tanks and our "open" test tank (with no aquatic life). The difference in temperature stability between the two test points was remarkable. Aquaponic life (in our case, tilapia) is durable and flexible, but rapid swings in water temperatures are very stressful and should be, as much as possible, avoided. Also, as a local research and development facility, it is our desire to fit in with the surrounding community in the best manner possible. Skirting the tanks has made the units a bit easier on the eyes, so to speak. If one is constructing an *Aqua-Pod* for interior use – greenhouse or artificial grow lighting – then the installation of skirts, like the installation of top covers, is not needed.

## 12.1 Tools required

- Electric drill with Phillips screw bit
- Hand-held reciprocating saw and scrolling blade

## 12.2 Materials required

- Two 4' × 8' treated wood siding
- 5/8" galvanized utility screws

## 12.3 Tanks/ponds skirt sizing and installation

**12.3.1** Installation of skirting is from the top of the corner support blocks to the top of the tank/pond top apron/skirt width support and the tank/pond top apron/skirt length support – items 2.3.12 and 2.3.13 respectively. There are a total of eight skirt panels to be manufactured and installed.
**12.3.2** Measure both end widths – approximately 51 ¼" – and scribe the measurement on a 4' × 8' panel. Cut a 51 ¼" piece.
**12.3.3** On the length of the 51 ¼" cut, scribe a 24" line and cut the panel in half lengthwise. The finished panel width is 22".

Cut 2" off either the center of each board or 2" off the outer edge of each board. The reason for this is, due to the textured surface of the panel, the seams will remain aligned and uniform throughout all eight apron/skirts installed.

**12.3.4** Install panels to both end widths with 5/8" galvanized screws.

**12.3.5** Side skirts consist of 6 panels – 4 at 22" x 34" and 2 at 22" x 36" (approximately). Take actual measurements and cut panels in the same manner as described in 12.3.2.

**12.3.6** Make cuts as described in 12.3.3 to maintain an aligned and uniform appearance and install with 5/8" galvanized screws.

*12.3 Apron/skirt Detail*

*In this, as in all phases of construction described here, check the actual measurements of components being sized and cut. A true fit may be ¼" off the dimensions cited here, and a check of the actual dimensions may well provide a stronger, tighter fit and look.*

### 13. Common Sense and Safety – BE SURE-BE SAFE-GET HELP!

1. **BE SURE!** Always take an actual measurement prior to making any cuts. The measurements contained herein are as close as we could get – particularly as concerns the basic *Aqua-Pod* outer frame. Remember – the tanks cannot be "shrunk" to fit. If there is any doubt as to the tanks fitting, put them into the frame and check for a fit prior to any final screwing/nailing.

2. **BE SURE!** Screwing versus nailing - At Cyrson Ranch Aquaponic Research and Development our first three *Aqua-Pods* were constructed with screws, permitting changes and modifications in prototype designs. The remaining two *Aqua-Pods* were constructed, for the most part, with a power nailer. Power nailing is a great time and money saver, and we suggest that you use a nailer when possible, except in places where screws are specifically recommended. It is important to follow the instructions for each component.

3. **BE SAFE!** Using a power nailer can be dangerous. The nails, on occasion, do not go where you would expect. Use eye protection. Move observers away from the work being nailed. Keep hands away from the back and edges of the piece being nailed.

4. **BE SAFE!** Use proper personal safety equipment. This includes wearing safety glasses on the construction site at

all times. Use gloves when necessary, and keep people out of the line of tools in use and any lengths of wood or pipe being moved and swung into place.

5.   **BE SAFE!** Inspect your tools. If a tool is not up to par, take it out of service until it can be repaired, sharpened, honed or replaced. When clamping, make sure the clamp is properly tightened. Before removing a clamp, check that the piece has been properly screwed/nailed.

6.   **BE SAFE!** Frayed electrical cords should be renewed or the tool replaced. Work from ground-protected outlets (GFI). Stop work if there is lightning or thunder in the area.

7.   **BE SAFE!** Working on ladders requires a spotter. No one should be airborne without an assistant on the ground whose sole responsibility is to protect the person above the ground.

8.   **BE SAFE!** Make it a point to understand the task at hand and how it is to be accomplished before starting any work. This manual contains detailed instructions for each aspect of the *Aqua-Pod* construction. If you have any question concerning proper procedures, stop and review the detailed instructions until the question is resolved.

9.   **GET HELP!** If construction of the aquaponics and *Aqua-Pod* is group project – school class, scout troop, community farm/garden – be sure to consider who is on site and what each person tasked to do. Too many people trying to work a project of this size can lead to poor results, at best; and to injuries, at worst. A great resource when "raising" an *Aqua-Pod* would be an experienced Habitat for Humanity volunteer operative. These people know a lot about putting things together with inexperienced participants and volunteers.

10. **GET HELP!** You can contact us here at CRA - aqua.podcra@gmail.com. We are happy to answer any questions and assist in any way we can!

## 14. Consolidated Materials and Costs Lists

### $75.98 - Ground cover: 6' x 100' polypropylene

### $155.56 - Frame Lumber, Pressure-Treated

- $27.88 - 2" x 6" – 10' cut to 7'2" – four @ $6.97
- $30.16 - 2" x 4" – 8' cut to 7'2" – eight @ $3.77
- $27.88 - 2" x 6" – 10' – four @ $6.97
- $13.94 - 2" x 6" – 10' cut to 59" – two @ $6.97
- $6.97 - 2" x 6" – 10' cut to 59" – one @ $6.97
- $9.94 - 2" x 4" – 10' cut to 59" – four @ $4.97
- $9.94 - 2" x 2" – 10' (ripped 2" × 4" to 1 ½" × 1 ¾") – two @ $4.97
- $9.94 - 2" x 4" – 10' – two @ $4.97
- $8.57 - 2" x 8" – 8' cut to 16" – one @ 8.57

### $44.26 - Fastening Hardware

- $27.48 - 2 ½" galvanized deck screws 5#
- $16.78 - 8d nails 5#

### $409.35 - Tanks/ponds Plumbing Materials

- $360.00 - Three tanks/ponds: Rubbermaid 150-gallon stock tanks #4245 @ $120
- $5.00 - Teflon tape for thread sealing $5.00 - Three sheets of sandpaper for cleaning PVC pipe cuts
- $2.93 - Three 1 ¼" male NPT (National Pipe Thread) to 1 ¼" socket PVC, schedule 40 straight adaptors @ $0.97

- $2.88 - Three 1 ¼" to ¾" reducing bushing – socket to socket PVC, schedule 40 @ $0.96
- $4.35 - Three ¾" / 10' runs of PVC pipe, schedule 40 @ 1.45
- $4.39 - Ten ¾" 90° EL sockets PVC, schedule 40, 25 pack
- $3.26 - Ten ¾" TEE sockets PVC, schedule 40, 10 pack
- $10.77 - PVC cleaner/primer, 16 oz.
- $10.77 - PVC glue, 16 oz.

## $214.91 - Grow Tubes

- $119.76 - Twelve runs of 4" x 10' schedule 20 PVC sewage line piping @ $9.98
- $49.20 - Twenty-four 4" PVC piping caps @ $ 2.05
- $9.72 - Twelve 90° EL's, ½" male NPT to ½" socket (street elbow) @ $0 .76
- $3.94 - Twelve 90° EL's, ½" socket to socket, ten pack @ $1.97
- $20.90 - Eight 10' runs, ½" schedule 40 PVC pipe @ $2.09
- PVC cleaner, previously accounted for
- PVC glue, previously accounted for
- Teflon tape, previously accounted for
- $11.99 - One tube – 3M Marine 5200 caulking

## $57.80 - Gravity Manifold

- $19.46 - One PVC Pipe schedule 40 – 4" x 10' cut to 44"
- $15.42 - Two PVC Pipe Caps schedule 40 – 4" diameter @ $7.71
- $21.72 - Twelve ½" male NPT to ½" barbed fitting @ $1.81
- $1.20 - One 90° EL, ½" male NPT to ½" barbed fitting
- Teflon tape, previously accounted for

- PVC cleaner, previously accounted for
- PVC glue, previously accounted for
- 2 ¼" galvanized screws, previously accounted for

## $12.83 - Weir Sump

- $4.97 - One 5-gallon weir bucket. An inexpensive trash can has been used because it offers a flat area to install the overflow piping with the least chance of leakage. History has proven that installations in round buckets (5-gallon "spackle bucket") can lead to leakage. These units have proven effective for 7(+) years with no headaches.
- ½" socket El, previously accounted for
- 4" run of ½" PVC pipe schedule 40, previously accounted for
- $0.56 - One ½" coupling socket to ½" threaded NPT
- $0.57 - One ½" coupling threaded ½" NPT
- $2.27 - One "O" ring that goes over the threads of the preceding (#5) item. This is the water seal, and it was arrived at by taking the ½" coupling and eyeballing "O" rings at the faucet area of the same store. Fortunately it worked the first time, and these are the dimensions: outside diameter = 1 3/32", inside diameter = 29/32", "O" ring thickness = 1/8". The exact dimensions aren't critical. Bear in mind the function required and go from there. If needed take the ½" coupling to the local auto supply store and have them size it with you. 10 pack
- $3.93 - Three pavers 12" x 12" @ $1.31

## $112.78 - Pump and Pump Sump

- $71.50 - One submersible pump – 205 GPH, 110V, 70 Watts (available at www.123ponds.com)
- $29.99 - One sump "series" operating float

- $2.85 - One 5-gallon utility bucket
- One 90° EL fitting – ½" female NPT to ½" barb, previously accounted for
- $4.99 - 6" electrical wire-tie wraps, 50 pack
- One 3' – ½" flexible PVC hose, previously accounted for
- $2.14 - 9/16" hose clamps, 10 pack
- $1.31 - One 12" × 12" paver

## $11.59 - Gravity Manifold Supply

- $2.09 - One 5' – ½" PVC pipe, schedule 20
- One 3' run of ½" flexible PVC, previously accounted for
- $1.12 - Two ½" couplings female socket to female NPT @ $0.56
- $2.40 - Two 90° EL's ½" male NPT to ½" barb fittings @ $1.20
- Two 9/16" "U" pipe straps, previously accounted for
- $5.98 - Four 1 ¼" utility screws, 1# box

## $79.07 - Gravity Manifold Feeds to Grow Tubes

- $35.57 - One 30' run of ½" flexible PVC tubing (sprinkler tubing), 50'
- $21.72 - Twelve ½" straight NPT to ½" barb fittings @ $1.81
- $9.24 - Twelve ½" NPT threaded caps with 1/8" hole drilled in cap center @ $0.77
- $12.54 - Twenty-four 3/8" to 7/8" hose clamps, 10 pack @ $4.18

## $92.45 - *Aqua-Pod* Top Cover: $92.45

- $5.97 - Fourteen #8 ½" lathe screws 260 screws
- $64.86 - Two 12' × 26" clear corrugated roofing panels (Tuflex – UltraVinyl) @ $32.43

- $21.62 - One 8' × 96" clear corrugated roofing panel (Tuflex – UltraVinyl)

## $57.44 - Tank/Ponds Apron/Skirts

- $57.44 - Two 4' x 8' treated wood siding @ $28.72
- 1 ¼" galvanized utility screws, previously accounted for

## $80.00 – Hybrid Soil-based Beds

- $80.00 - Eight barrels @ $10.00

## $1403.40 - Total Materials Costs*

* The prices of materials quoted here are "off the shelf" items as listed with several "box" store web sites in the Tampa Bay area of Florida. At Cyrson Ranch Research and Development all "new" items were used for quality assurance and to remove any doubt that a failure was the result of used, shoddy or faulty materials. That said, there is a wealth of inexpensive options available concerning materials gathering. As this is written there are two 150 gallon "Rubber Maid" tanks available for $50.00 each on Craig's List. There are numerous recycling yards springing up that offer PVC pipe and components at 15 cents on the dollar compared to new. Pumps are available for large savings as are system heaters through **outlets like Craig's List. The secret to buying "used" equipment is to** buy an excess number and always have a "spare" or two on hand to immediately place into service in the event of a failure. These used items are so inexpensive that the cost of purchasing an excess inventory is minimal compared to the security of 24/7/365 uninterrupted operations.

The above costs and pricing have been compiled, not to give the reader "sticker shock" but instead, to give the potential builder an *honest* assessment of true costs that are involved in the construction of the *Aqua-Pod* and related hybrid soil-based farm/garden. There remain a number of outfits that produce and sell aquaponic systems – mostly geared towards growing lettuce as a crop and fish – of varying size and complexity. A system somewhat resembling the *Aqua-Pod* production level (*without* the hybrid soil-beds and plant variety) costs, prior to shipping, somewhere in the $8950.00 range!!!

It is our opinion – at CRA R&D – that a similar system of durability and production cannot be constructed for much less, if any less at all, than the *Aqua-Pod* and garden presented herein.

*The development of the Aqua-Pod has been done to create an off-the-shelf aquaponic production platform available to anyone anywhere in the world. CRA R&D has approached the construction of the Aqua-Pod to entice people to build, operate and communicate an emerging technology with others working with an identical platform. The science of aquaponics must be developed and understood throughout the globe, and techniques must be communicated between involved parties to increase knowledge and acceptance as we continue to experience the death of traditional Big Ag operations due to ever-diminishing resources and supplies of water and fossil fuels, and the continuing results of constantly changing climate conditions.*

*Aquaponics – in any form – is not a part-time commitment. The systems must be maintained and it must be maintained the full year round. Whether operated and maintained by an individual, a class or through a community endeavor, the systems must be attended to during vacation, between terms or, God forbid, during an emergency or illness. When the decision has been made to pursue an aquaponic project it's important to network with others who are involved and knowledgeable of the practice. Aquaponic gardeners/farmers are a helpful lot, and when needed they will come. Do not be shy to ask for help. If nothing else, they can harvest the crop and find homes for the aquaculture if needed.*

\*\*\*

*Consider what's involved in aquaponics and gardening/farming. If you are not inclined toward working in the heat and the elements, getting wet, weeding, seeding, harvesting and fish mongering – don't get involved in aquaponics. It's hard work, but it's very rewarding. CRA R&D firmly believes the future of food production lies in aquaponic production, and it's important those who cleave to this path understand the important work they do and that they want to pursue this important work.*

## 15. Consolidated Tools List

- ½" NPT tap
- ¾" power bore drill bit
- 1 ¼" hole saw
- 1/8" drill bit
- 12' tape measure
- 12" crescent wrench
- 3 5/8" diameter hole saw
- Four clamps (Bar, F or Cam) – 0" to 12"
- 45/64" drill bit
- 5" hole saw
- 6 "C" clamps – 0" to 6"
- 6' step ladder
- 9/16" auger bit
- Aviation shears

- Carpenter's level – 3'
- Caulking gun
- Channel lock pliers
- Chop saw/Compound Miter – 14"
- Diagonal wire cutters
- Electric drill with Phillips head screwing bit
- Electric hand drill
- Electrical band saw
- Gloves
- Hack saw and blade
- Hammer – 16-ounce finishing
- Hand-held reciprocating saw and scrolling blade
- Large square – 2' x 3'
- Phillips head screwdriver
- Power drill press
- Power hacksaw
- Power nailer (Paslode)
- Sandpaper or emery cloth – medium grit
- Straight Edge – 1 yard
- Straight shank (blade) screwdriver
- Table saw
- Utility knife
- Wood cutting saw – 7 ¼' circular

If you are unfamiliar with any of these tools, use the internet or library for research. Most of these tools can be gathered and borrowed from throughout the community. Put the *Aqua-Pod* plan together and schedule construction dates. Go into the community – hobby clubs, senior citizen organizations, religious entities and educational/vocational centers – and ask for tools and assistance. A quality mission statement and a commitment to succeed will attract much-needed assistance and increase interest in aquaponic food production.

*It has been our intention at CRA R&D to design, build and create an aquaponic platform that brings the science to the world community as a whole. We do not assume the Aqua-Pod to be the most efficient production concept in aquaponics and we do not believe – at this time – such a system has been developed. The Aqua-Pod offers simplicity, durability and proven operational integrity. The Aqua-Pod platform is extremely flexible and very forgiving of mistakes or when certain conditions are missed or over looked.*

*aqua.podcra@gmail.com*

## VI. Starting the *Aqua-Pod* System and Creating the Bio-Filter

Before proceeding further we'll revisit the basics of aquaponics and how and why the system works. The following is a limited explanation, and I encourage you to further research the production of nitrates in nature and by industrial techniques. You may also want to revisit the section "Aquaponics Defined" found earlier in this manual.

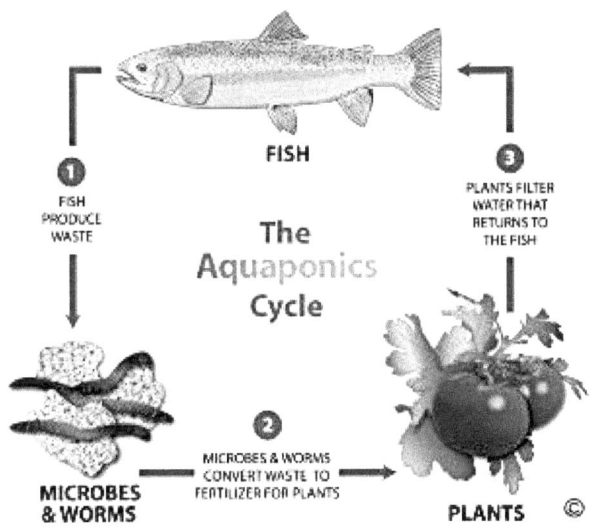

*Graphics Credit - TheAquaponicsSource.com*

## The bio-filter defined

Fish excrete ammonia through their bodies when they breathe (through their gills) and when they relieve themselves (excreta). Ammonia attracts the bacteria nitrosomonas, which convert the ammonia to nitrites. Nitrites attract the bacteria nitrospira, which convert the nitrites to nitrates. Nitrates are the major nutrient supply for vegetative growth in the system. Nitrates are carried to the grow tubes, where the plant roots take up the nutrition for growth.

I have read a number of definitions of a "bio-filter" and have come away, more often than not, confused. In reality the bio-filter lives throughout the unit and can best be described as the odorless slime one finds on the aquaponics platform unit components and on the fish themselves. The bio-filter "slime" is what makes live fish difficult to catch and handle. What is often termed the bio-filter is, in reality, a "reservoir" created to hold necessary bacteria – nitrosomonas and nitrospira – during fluctuating situations of fish density and weights, and plant size and quantity. The bio-filter can be any reservoir composed of a media that will provide for the production and storage of required bacteria to ensure constant stability of the overall health of the system. It is conceivable that a steadily operating aquaponics system – with no fluctuations – could be successfully operated without this reservoir.

The *Aqua-Pod* uses, as its bio-filter (reservoir), several thousand high-fired clay pellets dispersed throughout the 216 net pots in the grow-tube sockets. Creating a "reserve" bio-filter in this manner offers several advantages. Creating a bio-filter in the grow tubes negates the installation of a separate bio-filter unit and greatly increases the nutritional returns per area of space used. It also allows for removing the pellets and replacing them with clean dry pellets after a plant has "lived out" and is removed from the unit (pellets can be cleaned, dried and reused). With this method, the bio-filter never grows old and ineffective and, it eliminates the chance of bio-filter collapse or the requirement that the bio-filter be removed from service for mass cleaning; leaving the unit without a bio-filter "reserve" during the cleaning period. This method provides bio-filter strength, durability, flexibility and great ease of operation.

## Start-up requirements and system monitoring

- Water requirements
- pH monitoring
- Temperature monitoring
- Water clarity
- Odor
- Total dissolved solids (TDS) monitoring
- Fish stock – selecting a fish type for start-up
- Plant/vegetation stock – selecting and seeding for start-up
- Tending to the system during start-up

## Water requirements

Chlorinated water can be detrimental to aquatic life. Most municipal water is chlorinated to sterilize the water and this is achieved by one of two means – adding chlorine or chloramines. Chlorine can be "gassed" off over a period of time, or more rapidly by agitating, but chloramines can be removed only by the addition of a sodium thiosulfate-based solution. Upon the initial establishment of the CRA R&D center we researched the municipal water available and found that, of the five pumping stations in the county, only one was using chloramines (not the station serving our site). As it was clear the county had no hard and fast rule against using chloramines (as do some municipalities), we decided to use a sodium thiosulfate-based solution in a liquid concentrate to take out both chlorine and chloramines. It was a good decision because on several occasions since start-up the water at our station has, in fact, been treated with chloramines. The concentrated product used is inexpensive, nontoxic, easy to use and very affective. Fill each 150-gallon tank/pond and add the concentrated liquid chlorine/chloramines remover as the manufacturer's label indicates.

*This is a good time to mention "Material Safety Data Sheets" (MSDS). Most, if not all, of the additives one might use in aquaponics; pesticides, herbicides, fertilizers – organic or not – are required to have a MSDS enclosed with the product or available on the internet as the label directs (the same applies to oils, paints, fuels, soaps and detergents…). There are 15 sections of a MSDS; safe handling, fire fighting measures, storage, reactivity… to name a few. Of particular importance to the aquaponics operator is section 12 – "Ecological Information" - an analysis of the effects of the substance on fish, honeybees and worms (along with some other items). If you are not familiar with MSDS's take some time to get an understanding of what they offer. The information within may well help you to decide what you want to use in your garden specifically and, generally, in your life as a whole.*

Do not use water from ponds, streams or rivers as it may have pathogens from the excretions of warm-blooded mammals. If municipal treated water is not available, make every effort to use water from a "source" supply, such as spring water, captured rain or clean melted snows.

Fill the tank/ponds, and note the levels. Regularly check the level and observe any loss of water. There will be some evaporation, but it will be in the area of one gallon (tops) per 24 hours. Keep in mind that the *Aqua-Pod* design is foolproof as the tank/ponds cannot be pumped dry. But if the piping construction is compromised due to poor installation, the water can leak out and destroy the aquaculture. *Now is the time to determine system integrity!*

Once system integrity is confirmed, run up the pump and add water to the sump as the gravity manifold and grow tubes fill. The system is fully operational when the sump is full, the tank/ponds are topped, and water is returning from the tank/ponds to the weir and overflowing to the pump sump.

## pH Monitoring

Monitor the pH at each step. pH is the most important test available in monitoring an aquaponic system. Take a baseline pH immediately following the initial introduction of water to the tanks/ponds, following the addition of the chlorine/chloramines remover and several times per day as the bio-filter develops and the system begins to "cycle" properly. Changes in pH may not occur rapidly, but understanding the baseline and monitoring it throughout the process is important. A properly cycling system has a pH of 7.0 to 7.6.

## Temperature monitoring

Temperature monitoring is important because high swings in pH levels can occur with temperature changes of the water. Temperature also affects the ability of the water to hold oxygen and changes the O2 content. Rapid drops in the water temperature can cause organics in the system tank/ponds to draw off available O2 and a fish kill can occur. Keep a close eye on the water temperature and be aware of how and what it affects. Like any farmer you'll be watching the weather

## Water clarity

Use a clear plastic device – a clear jar or plastic tumbler. At CRA R&D, we a use small rectangular plastic tank. Regardless of what you choose, use the same method all the time. Take a sample from the tank/ponds and hold it up to the light; put your thumb up on the other side and rate how well you can see your thumb. In a properly cycling system clarity will be clear with a slight copper-colored hue.

*Water Clarity Check*

## Odor

An ammonia odor can be a good indication of problems developing. It can indicate a fish kill or the threat of one developing. If odors are evident, check the pH immediately and measure the TDS and the water temperature. Try to determine which tank/pond the odor is emanating from and drag the bottom of the tank to discover any dead fish. If there is no evidence of a kill, proceed with a one third change-out of the entire system; refill with de-chlorinated water and continue to monitor. If the odor persists, pump the entire system down and remove the fish to a holding tank. Inspect and clean all tank/ponds, refill with de-chlorinated water and return the fish, evenly distributing them among the tanks. You may find that you simply have too many fish and need to harvest few of the larger fish (and have a yummy dinner).

*Clarity and smell may seem like simple items with little need for discussion. I bring these into the mix to suggest that you trust your instincts and use the "basics" as the first steps in analysis.*

## Total dissolved solids (TDS)

TDS doesn't impart a lot of information to the aquaponics operator. But it is an indication of change, and a large movement can suggest that problems might be developing. Test the tap water as a baseline, and test the TDS on a daily basis. Tap water baseline at the CRA R&D site is about 210 ppm. The systems run about 275 ppm and a one third change-out is accomplished at no greater 320 ppm. Because we use the effluent to feed hybrid soil-based plants (performing a 20 percent change-out twice per week) there is seldom the need to do a mandatory transfer of one third of the system due to a 320 ppm TDS reading.

### *Testing Reagents and Meters*

*A number of tools are available to fill the system monitoring toolbox. You can test ammonia, nitrites, nitrate and oxygen content. There are titration test kits and some rather expensive meters available. It is good to have available kits for ammonia, nitrites, nitrates and oxygen testing when bringing the unit on-line. Take baseline tests immediately following introduction of the water to the tank/ponds, and retake the tests once the cycle is established. If needed, take samples and test while establishing the bio-filter; a word of caution: Don't "chase" the results (particularly pH) by getting overly excited and adding balancers that create "swing" results. It takes three to six weeks to establish the bio-filter and achieve proper cycling. During this period the greatest concern is keeping the environment balanced for the fish to survive.*

*An Example of Meters and Reagents Available*

## Starting the System at CRA

*When establishing the initial bio-filter at the CRA R&D center we monitored – several times daily – the pH levels, clarity, TDS and odor. In week four we experienced a radical drop in clarity, an increase in odor, an increase in TDS (up to 360 ppm) and a rise in pH (to 8.9). We frantically but gently (remember, in the beginning we had very little idea of what we were doing) started treating the system with distilled white vinegar, bringing the pH down 0.1 to 0.2 per day. In ten days the system was clear, pH was in the 7.0 range, the odor was gone and TDS was 280 ppm. The bio-filter was established and the system was cycling properly. Since establishing the initial bio-filter with 300 gallons of water we have used this to feed four new system start-ups, with no bio-filter issues in any of the units. This leads me to suggest that the new aquaponics platform operator seek out other established operations that may be able to provide "starter" bio-filter to ease the start-up symptoms in new systems.*

There is further discussion of monitoring techniques elsewhere in this manual. What is been presented here are the basics in understanding, monitoring and correction during the initial start-up phase.

## Fish stock – selecting a fish for start-up

For the initial start-up CRA R&D used goldfish "feeder" stock. These are an inexpensive, hardy fish sold in aquarium hobby stores to feed to carnivorous aquarium fish – piranha and the like. Initially we had 100 of these small fish, and they proved well up to task to create the initial bio-filter and get the system cycling. Once the system was balanced and plants were growing and producing, the goldfish were isolated to one tank and tilapia "fry" were introduced. Goldfish and tilapia eat different foods, and both were kept on hand for each species. The goldfish have long ago been given away for aquariums, and now tilapia is the sole species grown at CRA R&D.

*Gold Fish used in Start-up of First Unit*

Tilapia is a healthy, tasty, feisty fish with, if it may even be considered in a fish, a fun personality. At feeding time they are quite active and often appear to want to "splash" the feeder. If that's the case, it is rather endearing. Tilapias are cichlids and are mouth breeders. The female carries the fertilized eggs in her mouth until they hatch; they are then introduced into the tank/pond environment. They are very prolific, and at last count we had, in 15 tanks/ponds of 2,250 gallons, 453 fish of 1" to 17" in length and an estimated 1000(+) fry. It should be noted that two to six fish are harvested for food weekly.

To acquire our tilapia, CRA R&D used Craig's List and traveled to Orlando from Tampa to pick up 100 of what are better termed as "fingerlings" (¼"). We have never had to purchase fish again and, on several occasions have given fry, fingerlings and fish (along with bio-filter water) to other aquaponic start-ups.

### *About our "Starter Fish"*

*Our goldfish fish were so friendly they would swim up to the surface and nibble a person's fingers. They wiggled about and "danced" and ate out of the feeder's hand. Some of these fish would let you "pet" them. For the first 26 months the of R & D we monitored a sampling of the system fish in five 55-gallon glass aquarium tanks along with ten 10-gallon "medical" tanks (which we never needed). Kids would visit and fall in love with our goldfish. We slowly parted with both goldfish and medical tanks as these were taken by the children. We will occasionally receive word and a picture of a rather large goldfish that we initially purchased at ¼" to ½" in length.*

## Plants and vegetation – selecting and seeding for start-up

Start-up requires enough plants and vegetation to take up the ammonia, nitrites and ultimately nitrates while developing the bio-filter and achieving a proper cycle. Plants will take up little ammonia and not much more in nitrites, but they are required to develop a bio-filter. Specific plant stock, and plants suggested for start-up, is further discussed in the section "Plant Selection, Acquisition and Seeding."

**Pots:** Using a "net" pot 3 ¾" in diameter, with an upper lip extending to 4", is the perfect size in the *Aqua-Pod* design. CRA R&D uses the Gro Pro 3.75 pot (#724510 at Sunlight Supply, www.sunlightsupply.com). Acquire 100 pots for start-up. Most hydroponic shops and suppliers have these net pots available.

**Vegetation growth medium:** High-fired, light-weight clay pellets are the best medium for aquaponic growth. The pellets are inexpensive, and they can be cleaned and reused. They are approximately 3/8" in diameter and can be found at most hydroponic supply stores and at Sunlight Supply. This medium offers several important qualities. Most important is the ability to periodically renew the pebble base with a clean, dry medium. When a plant has played out its life, the net pot is emptied and clean pebbles are used for replanting. Using this method of renewing portions of the bio-filter on a constantly rotating basis negates the shutdown of a central consolidated bio-filter for mass cleaning. Any time the entire bio-filter is taken out of service; there is the chance that the system will be compromised. The pebbles also provide a strong seeding base for transfer to the hybrid soil beds. Using Jiffy Pods, set into the upper portion of the net pots, you can start a seed in the *Aqua-Pod* and then remove it to plant in the soil. Our research reveals that seed propagation in the *Aqua-Pod* returns a significantly greater rate of success compared to soil-based propagation, and all of our seed start-ups are done in the *Aqua-Pod's.*

We do not recommend using a "wool" medium because, for the most part, wool is a one-use item, and it develops an algae buildup. If you are using a wool product, be sure it's sterile and doesn't have fertilizers entrained that might be harmful to the aquatic life. CRA R&D has also found that gravel and sand media in hybrid soil-based beds create excessive algae growth, which competes with plant growth.

*Many of the products and items available to the aquaponic farmer have been designed for the much larger field of hydroponics. Whether or not you believe that hydroponics is a viable, renewable food source (CRA R&D does not support hydroponics because it is simply another polluting, artificially fertilizing and high-energy-use farming technique), you must be aware of adverse chemicals and fertilizers that may compromise a balanced bio-filter. Be aware of what your aquaponic system is subjected to at all times!*

**Starting the vegetation:** Clean the pebble medium by spreading it out on concrete; wash it with fresh water and let it dry. Select hardy plants for initial start-up, and if possible seed the plant. Jiffy starter pods are excellent for starting seed and can be ordered inexpensively in 1,000 piece lots. Some seeds – okra, basil, onion, beet, cilantro, marigold (any large seed) – can be started in the net pots, but they must be placed low enough to leach moisture yet high enough not to drown. Parsley, celery, and lettuces – because they are small seeds – are best started in a Jiffy Pod where they can remain in the *Aqua-Pod* or be removed to the soil beds. Great shoots to cultivate are Cuban oregano, aloe and pineapple. "Box-store" plants can also be used if some of the dirt is removed by shaking it away; cherry tomatoes are a good box-store plant, as are herbs and spices if you don't seed those. Some dirt (the Jiffy Pods can be placed directly into net pots with the clay medium) is tolerable; just keep it to a minimum. If the grow tubes get too much dirt in them, evacuate the plants, take the tube out of the system, hose it out until clean and replace it in service.

Jiffy Pod seeding in net pots with high-fired clay pellets is a simple process with great returns. Once a Jiffy Pod is hydrated, its dimensions are 1 ¼" in diameter and 1 ¼" in height, place the Jiffy

Pod and pebbles in the net pot, with the Jiffy Pod 5/8" above the top layer of pebbles. Seed the Jiffy Pod and then dunk the net pot in a tank/pond up to the upper rim of the net pot. This jump starts the leaching of the effluent/moisture up to the seed. Place the net pot in a *Aqua-Pod* grow tube socket.

*Plants from nurseries and box stores come with bugs in them, and the grower needs to remain aware of this. At CRA R&D we re-seed and "shoot off" 95 percent of our plant stock (we have many multi-generations aquaponic seed lines). When we do introduce a new plant it is treated with AzaMax – outside of, and away from, the unit – before it is placed into the Aqua-Pod (or into the hybrid soil-bed systems). Further discussion about AzaMax and pest control can be found elsewhere in this manual.*

When collecting seed, stick with open-pollinated plant varieties rather than hybrids as hybrids do not always come back "true" when re-seeding.

Our R & D recommendation for start-up – the *"workhorses"* of the plant *"take-up"* family – are Cuban oregano and aloe. Place one net pot of Cuban oregano and one net pot of aloe in each grow tube. If other plants are available place them in service – but the minimum calls for 12 of each; Cuban oregano and aloe. Get some seeds going in the Jiffy Pods, and transfer what you have available into net pots. The Cuban oregano and aloe will "work" the system while the bio-filter is developed, and by the time the cycle is reached there will be plenty of vegetation to build system strength. See the section "Plant Selection, Acquisition and Seeding" for in-depth information discussing the many vegetation options for both the *Aqua-Pod* use and hybrid soil-based, aquaponically fed methods.

## Tending to the system during start-up

With all elements in place – fish, plants and proper circulation – tending to the system commences. Feed the fish a good-quality food once daily. If you are working with tilapia fry, the food will need to be ground in a coffee/spice grinder to a fine powder. If you have fingerlings, use a coarse grind. Goldfish flakes are adequate for mature goldfish, but break them up for small fish. Do not over feed the tank/ponds – not in the start-up cycling period and not once the bio-filter is established. Remove any floating food ten minutes after feeding. Monitor the pH, water temperature, water clarity, odor and total dissolved solids. Needless to say, this is not a good time to take a vacation. Spend the next three to six weeks working with the plants and the garden layout, reading this manual and going on the internet to research and discover more information, contacts and resources available about aquaponic farming.

*You are now an aquaponic farmer/engineer – welcome!*

*This section on monitoring has been adequate to get your Aqua-Pod properly cycling with a healthy bio-filter. There is further discussion elsewhere in this manual concerning monitoring and correction if needed. At Cyrson Ranch Aquaponics Research and Development, we spent the first 26 months maintaining a precise accounting of developments, ambient environment, weather conditions, system conditions and aquatic life health. Operating an interior lab with five 55-gallon glass tanks and ten 10-gallon fry tanks and medicine tanks, we were better able to see how the fish were progressing and living in the systems, and we were able to address any impending issues. Throughout the remainder of this manual we will address these and later findings to help you achieve success in operating your Aqua-Pod.*

## VII. Soil-Based Bed Installation

It's important to take the time to discuss "soil" and what it is in a naturally occurring state and what it has become through the use of synthetic fertilizers, pesticides and herbicides used in large industrial agriculture. Suffice it to say, what has been done to the soils throughout the "modern" world – and much of the third world – has resulted in a drastic change in composition and quality. I like to imagine the two substances – natural and industrial - and define them as such: **SOIL** is a healthy amalgam of naturally occurring humus, beneficial bacteria, actinomycetes (manures), fungi (molds, mushrooms), algae, micro-fauna (nematodes, protozoa, rotifers) and macro fauna (worms, spiders, beetles, springtails, flies, termites, ants, centipedes, slugs and larval forms of moths and butterflies) with added nutrients from composting and, in the case of the *Aqua-Pod* garden, nitrates transferred from the unit bio-filter, and; **DIRT**, the result of industrial farming methods that kill and destroy most, if not all, of the naturally occurring beneficial elements found in **SOIL**.

Venture, if permitted (*and I strongly doubt you will receive permission*), onto a large industrial operation and scoop a handful of two of dirt from several locations. You will find no worms or other active insect life. The dirt does not smell of fresh humus. The dirt the industrial plant is raised in has little relation to *soil* and requires copious amounts of synthetic fertilizers to provide the nourishment needed to grow plants. Herbicides have killed plants that would naturally be used as compost and all micro-fauna and macro-fauna have been destroyed with pesticides. The reality of industrialized agriculture raises an important question: *If insects and other plants can't exist in the production of our food, is the food safe to consume?*

Dirt used by large industrial agriculture, and the way it is treated, is a result of analysis in "reductionist science" with its beginnings in the early 20th century. "Reductionism" assumes that everything can be understood by reducing it to its simplest components. The conclusion of this analysis, as it relates to plant growth, is that there are three simple inorganic factors required – nitrogen, phosphates and potassium – and little else, if anything else at all, is further needed. In the short term this may be true. But in the longer term what we have found is the need to treat the dirt with ever increasing amounts of these three components and there is the question that there may come a time when the dirt no larger suffices to achieve adequate growth regardless of how heavily it is treated. When that time arrives – either through the inability to further produce and treat at ever increasing levels or upon reaching a saturation *"end-point"* – massive swaths of land used in current industrialized farming methods will become untenable. The land will then be deserted, ignored and left to erode with *"dust-bowl"* results.

Synthetic nitrogen owes its existence to war and the munitions industry. The "Haber" process – used in the production of today's fertilizer – was originally discovered by Fritz Haber in 1909 when he was able to produce ammonia from the air – a highly complex energy consuming process. The Haber method processed ammonia is oxidized and converted to nitric acid providing the basis of explosives such as ammonium nitrate, nitro-glycerin and trinitrotoluene (TNT). It is estimated that munitions created with ammonia in this manner has resulted in the deaths of between 100 and 150 million people in wars of the 20th century.

Though the effects upon crops of nitrates was known, or rather "sensed", for thousands of years it wasn't until the 18th century that ammonia, and the resultant nitrates, were identified as an important aspect of plant growth and, more importantly, accelerated plant growth. Justas von Liebig introduced the concept of analysis that the process could be simplified through the use of inorganic compounds. Von Liebig was, perhaps, the first of the "reductionist" to enter the field of agriculture.

The end of both world wars idled large weapons production facilities. Governments and industries quickly shifted into the fertilizer production mode and subsidized farms and farmers who used the fertilizer in crop production. These steps ensured increased demand, solid profits and the continued ability to shift production back to munitions manufacturing when needed. This also, following WWII in particular, firmly established the "industrial agri-business" giants and signaled the impending doom to the vast majority of small "family" farms.

I won't go any further into detail of the history or scientific analysis of the soil. That will be a large focus in the second of the series *"Aquaponics in a Changing World"* and the detailed section: "Own the Soil". What follows are detailed instructions on the *how's* and *why's* of creating your own healthy hybrid soil-beds for your *Aqua-Pod* garden.

Two following points have guided CRA in the decision to install hybrid soil-based garden beds:

- Our original mission statement requires that the system provide an operating platform with the greatest nutritional value and return, durability and longevity, the least use of water and power, flexibility and variety in plants produced and a high level of control by the system operator. The first unit, "Pee Wee", a system with two 150-gallon tanks, was designed and built in the wake of the attacks by Israel on residents of the Gaza Strip in 2008. With the encroaching "wall(s)" being constructed in and around Gaza and with residents' movement limited, it became apparent that someone needed to develop a locally based system that uses a minimum of water and can be located at, or very near, the home to provide food in a war-torn environment. Feeding soil-based plants is a requirement of a functioning system in this case.

- Growing fish for food, or as ornamentals, creates excess effluents of ammonia, nitrites and nitrates. Tampa Bay is one of the leading areas of the world in the production of ornamental fish for the aquarium hobbyist. Prior to initiating our own work, CRA R&D was able to visit a number of ornamental fish farms and observe practices and habits. One issue we found with every visit was the difficulty of filtering and reducing excess levels of effluent in managing a healthy (and profitable) aquaculture operation. Some filtering attempts were quite involved, and others were simply a matter of pumping it into the waste stream. Though no operation we visited was an aquaponic farm, we assumed that our operation would also require some management of excessive nitrates (a balanced bio-filter) as not all the nitrates can be taken up by the vegetation in the grow tubes (or so we assumed). The problem was that we had no idea how much nitrate would be generated. The system had to be built, installed and analyzed. We decided to incorporate hybrid soil-based, aquaponically fed, operations to ensure the balance of nitrates as the numbers were developed and analyzed.

It took close to three and a half years to gather and develop the initial data and conclusions. Immediately starting the project we sized eight barrels per *Aqua-Pod*, placed them into service and observed they provided excellent returns. Analysis indicated that a 20 percent "change-out" twice per week (180 gallons) generated 1.55 pounds (0.71 Kg) of nitrates per year per *Aqua-Pod*. Excess nitrates – whether from aquaponic (fish-based) operations or from manufactured fertilizers – can be devastating to inland streams, lakes and rivers, as can be seen throughout Florida and much of the USA. As it remains our commitment to minimize any "run-off" effects that an *Aqua-Pod* operation might contribute to this problem, we decided to increase the soil-based footage by 50 percent, bringing the total square footage per each *Aqua-Pod* to 12 barrel units (37.3 square feet).

*CRA has some experience working with hydroponics and hydroponics does provide a method of plant production. However, we do not consider it an alternative to industrial Big Ag nor do we consider it "organic." The energy used, the ingredients involved and the resultant residuals are as harmful to the environment – and the consumer - as any large mechanized industrial farm operation. Furthermore CRA does not consider hydroponics a sustainable method of food production.*

The hybrid soil-based systems at CRA are hydroponic methods, but instead of using plant *"food"* and *"nutrition"* – manufactured using fossil fuels and packed with industrially produced nitrates and chemicals – the aquaponic method uses the naturally produced nitrates from a balanced aquaponic bio-filter. The soil, treated to assist plant growth with naturally occurring products of potassium, lime, magnesium, iron, manure, micronutrients and organic compost, encourages the addition and growth of beneficial bacteria, fungi, micro-fauna and macro-fauna.

> *Today's agricultural methods are exhausting and polluting our soil and water. Industrial agriculture uses 70 percent of the planet's fresh water. According to the EPA, US agriculture contributes to nearly 75 percent of all water-quality problems in the nation's rivers, lakes and streams.*

The *Aqua-Pod* garden uses 6 percent – or less – of the water used in industrial farming methods. The *Aqua-Pod* garden has no adverse effect on our lakes, streams or rivers.

To assist the reader in layout techniques the following drawing depicts the layout of the CRA operation. Essentially five times larger in scope than a single *Aqua-Pod* garden, it incorporates all the essentials discussed in this manual. Note the ground cover and close proximity of the hybrid soil-based planters. The initial plant beds were installed prior to the development of the time-saving mechanical plant with transfer pump, piping and cross connections to the municipal water supply. Feeding/watering rates in an operation of this size are flexible and may consist of 10 percent to 35 percent "change-outs" depending on aquaculture density, humidity, rain conditions and crop maturity. If rain frequency drops to unsustainable levels some soil-based beds are harvested, and the beds remain fallow until the rains return. You can read more about the CRA farm in the "Farm Layout - Growing Your Operation" section of this manual.

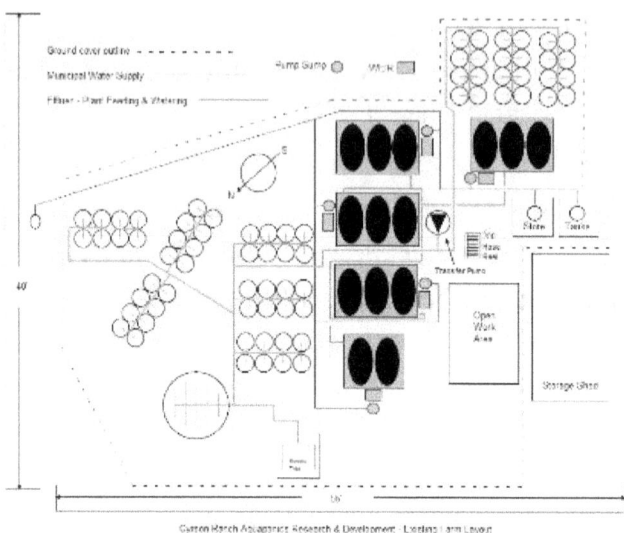

Ground cover outline – – – – – – –
Municipal Water Supply
Filter - Plant Feeding & Watering ――――――

Pump Sump

Cyrson Ranch Aquaponics Research & Development - Loading Farm Layout

*Farm Layout at Cyrson Ranch Aquaponics Research and Development*

## 7.0 Sighting the Soil-based Garden

Lay a double layer of ground cover – 5' x 12'. (You can size better after completing the section "Barrel Construction and Modification") It's important to lay ground cover for ease of maintenance and to isolate the barrels from the native soil. If you are working any place like Florida, you need to keep local pests out of the soil beds or you'll be fighting a constant losing battle. The soil placed into use is created by the operator and should initially be sterilized and bagged or drenched with an organic pesticide such as AzaMax.

*As operators in southwest Florida we are aware that those unfamiliar with the location often get the idea that Florida is a "breadbasket" location in farm production because it's assumed to be hospitable to farming and plant production. That's not true. Yes, Florida produces vast amounts of fruits and vegetables but at incredible costs in imported soils, water, fuel, fertilizer, pesticides and herbicides (and human suffering). To get a clear picture of what is required to grow industrially in Florida, read "Tomatoland" by Barry Estabrook (Andrew McMeel Publishing 2011). You may never buy another winter tomato again.*

## 7.1 Barrel Construction and Modification

## Tools required

- Drill
- 3/8" drill bit
- 1/4" drill bit
- Hand-held reciprocating saw
- Wood/plastic saw blade

## Materials required

- Six plastic 55-gallon food-grade barrels. (These barrels can be sourced used through places like Craig's List).

## Barrel modifications

**7.1.1** The barrel is molded with a seam about two fifths of the distance from the top and another two fifths from the bottom.
**7.1.2** On the lower seam drill a 3/8" hole.

*7.1.2 Drill a 3/8" Hole Prior to Cutting the Barrel*

**7.1.3** Using the hand-held reciprocating saw, work around the barrel and cut on the seam until the lower portion is separated. Get assistance if needed.

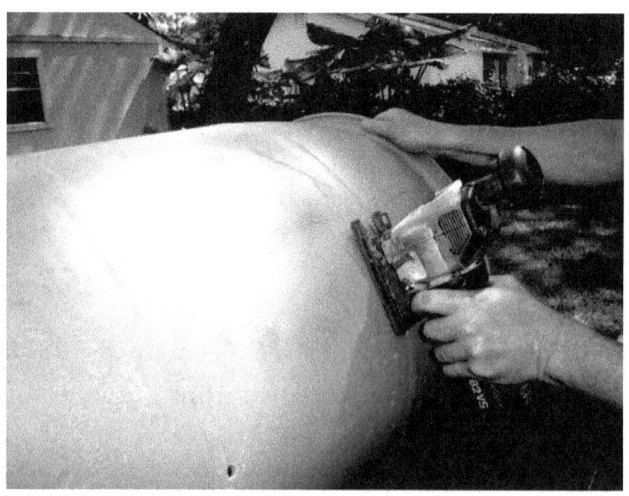

*7.1.3 Cut the Barrel along the Molded Seam*

**7.1.4** Repeat with the upper part of the barrel; discard the middle excess.

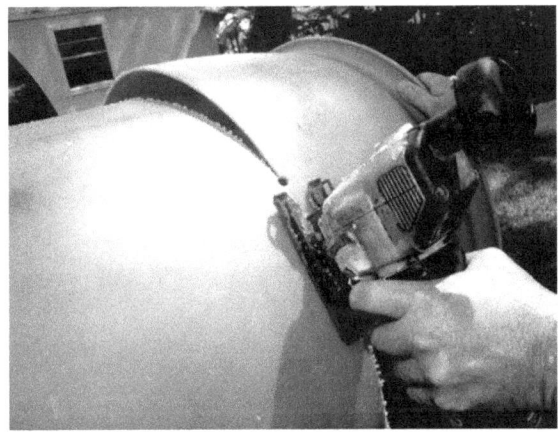

*7.1.4 Cut the Barrel along the opposite Molded Seam*

**7.1.5** At 1" to 2" from the base of each barrel half, use the 1/4" drill bit to drill holes 2" apart around the entire circumference. These are the sole drainage for the tanks (and the sole entry points for any pests).

*7.1.5 Drill Drainage Holes in the Barrel*

**7.1.6** Arrange the barrels in two rows (side by side) of four in length on the ground cover.

*7.1.6 Example of Barrel Layout (note the "piped" irrigation)*

**7.1.7** Make any changes in ground cover positioning, and the staple the cover.

## 7.2 Creating Your Soil

The following amalgam created addresses the following needs of plants:

- Primary Ingredients – Nitrogen, Phosphorous, Potassium.
- Secondary Ingredients – Calcium, Magnesium, Sulfur.
- Trace Nutrients – Boron, Chlorine, Cobalt, Copper, Iron, Manganese, Molybdenum, Nickel, Sodium, Zinc.

To provide these soil components I have laid out the following additives, what they provide for the soil, and the amounts to mix together and place into the hybrid soil-beds. I also include specific brand names. It's sad, and enlightening, that when the decision is made to work with a true organic soil and one sets out to arrive at the elements required to make good soil, they are immediately confronted with how the market has been cornered by the big industrial fertilizer manufacturers. Walk into a "box" store and try to purchase the elements as listed below and you will come up well short of anything used in this manual - it's simply unavailable at the "box" store outlets.

*Be very careful purchasing in main stream outlets because you will find, however cleverly concealed, additives and amendments that compromise a good organic soil and that will destroy the natural development of bacteria, actinomycetes, fungi, algae, micro-fauna and macro fauna.*

Unless otherwise indicated all element and components listed were purchased through "Worms Way" stores. There are five throughout the USA and one of them is located in the Tampa Bay area that CRA calls home. It is not my intention to "drive" the reader to any specific outlet for the purchase of the items used. The internet has a number of outlets that sell these same, and very similar, products and you are urged to explore the possibilities available. You may find, as I did, that there are other alternative products that will work as well as those I suggest - just be sure your soil has the elements and components outlined here.

There are some items listed that are of questionable sustainability and I will touch on those as we proceed. Not everything used at CRA can be considered "sustainable" though we continue to work towards that goal. Our purpose is to enlighten the reader, and the world as a whole, to the methods and the positive results of aquaponics – and the *Aqua-Pod* specifically – gardening techniques.

## Tools required

- Spade shovel
- Coal shovel
- Wheel barrow
- Pitch fork – four tine spading is best
- Gloves

## Materials required

*Soil Components*

- 36 – 40 pound bags of soil. Purchase the least expensive at a "box" store. This provides the "base" to your blend. This component comes without any bugs or pests (hopefully – check before using) and can be a great help in initially establishing your soil without local "critters" that might be harmful.

- Straw – one bale; or, if you can get it without cost, Spanish moss. We have found Spanish moss to be a great pest inhibitor. Through local observation we deduced it would provide *some* protection but it has performed well beyond our expectations.

- Sterilized cow manure – the least expensive is fine. It's important to stay away from raw manures from "warm blooded" animals because of the potential bacterial harm to humans that can occur upon consumption of foods tainted with it. Any sterilized manure is useful. I mention sterilized cow manure because it is easy to get at a low price.

- Pro-Mix H.P. Mycorrhizae - provides a superior growing environment for plants that require increased drainage and oxygen. In addition to Canadian sphagnum peat moss, perlite, major- and micro-nutrients, dolomite and calcitic limestone, it's fortified with beneficial endomycorrhizal fungus to strengthen roots and increase plants' ability to fully utilize available nutrients. 3.8 cubic feet of compressed Pro-Mix equals about seven cubic feet in use and provides the bulk, along with the purchased soil, to the hybrid plant beds.

- Earthworm Castings - earthworm castings rival chemical fertilizers in their nutrient composition by providing a concentrated source of calcium, magnesium and nitrogen, as well as many trace minerals and growth hormones. It is supplied in 15 pound bags.

- Bone Meal – A source of organic phosphorus and nitrogen. Bone Meal is also "injected" into the soil to promote healthy flowering. "Injection" will be discussed further in this section. It is supplied in 10 pound bags. Bone Meal is available at "box" stores but is quite expensive.

- Greensand - a naturally occurring iron-potassium silicate that can hold ten times its weight in moisture; it contains over 30 trace minerals. Mined from deposits in the U.S. the sustainability of greensand can be questioned though it is marketed as sustainable. It is supplied in 7 ½ pound bags.
- Azomite - is a natural mineral product that has been mined in Utah for more than 60 years. It contains a broad spectrum of over 70 metabolically active minerals and trace elements. The sustainability of Azomite can be, like that of Greensand, questioned. It is supplied as a granular in 10 pound bags.
- Biochar (Black Gold Charcoal) – is a recently "rediscovered" soil amendment that can increase soil fertility of acidic soils (low pH soils), increase agricultural productivity, and provide protection against some foliar and soil-borne diseases. It has the ability to capture and hold large amounts of substances including water and carbon dioxide. Biochar is under investigation as an approach to carbon sequestration to produce negative carbon dioxide emissions. All organic farmers should be using Biochar in their soil amendments. Biochar is supplied in 2 qt. bags but can be made very inexpensively by pulverizing a "natural" charcoal. "Cowboy Brand" hardwood lump charcoal is available throughout the USA and we have used that on numerous occasions. DO NOT use commercial charcoal "briquettes". I would also strongly urge that you do not use bio-char as a component of your aquaponics system bio-filter until more research has been done.

*The use of the above listed materials in making your hybrid soil-based beds yield a quality humus and loam while, at the same time, providing excellent secondary and trace nutrients. With the addition of nitrates from the Aqua-Pod effluent and waste composting, and with the attraction of micro-fauna and macro-fauna, a healthy pest resistant soil base is created to provide optimal returns in an organic manner.*

## 7.3 Making Up the Soil-based Beds

- With the beds set in place take and place several handfuls of straw - or Spanish moss - at the bottom of each. The straw permits some air passages at the bottom and will compost over time.

*Add a Layer of Spanish Moss in the Bottom of the Barrel*

- Place two bags of soil into each bed and dampen. Punch vertical holes into the soil using the pitch fork. DO NOT PUNCH THROUGH THE BOTTOM OF THE BARREL.

*Two Bags of Soil, Dampen and Aerate*

- In a wheel barrow place approximately 1/12th of the Pro-Mix H.P., and several handfuls of each: Azomite, Bone Meal, Worm Castings and Greensand. Add one handful of Charcoal. Add the third bag of soil (soil is helpful at this level because worms need soil for proper digestion). With the spade mix thoroughly.

*Mix the Soil Aggregates*

- Top the soil in the bed with the previously mixed components and dampen. Punch the beds again to aerate with the pitchfork.

*Fill the Barrel*

*Aerate the Soil*

- If you have good compost on hand put an inch on top followed by an inch of cow manure. Punch again with the pitchfork.

*Add Manure and Compost*

- Top the bed with a handful or two of straw - or Spanish moss - and wet heavily.

*Top the Barrel with Moss and Water*

- Repeat for the remaining eleven hybrid soil beds.
- "AzaMax" is a natural pesticide and is OMRI (the Organic Manufacturer Review Institute) certified and, though it is expensive, it is a very effective pest deterrent. It can be used as a *"drench"* or as a spray. If you suspect you may have some local pests entrained in your soil mix add two tablespoons to one to two gallons of water and *"drench"* each barrel accordingly. The use of AzaMax is discussed several times throughout this manual.

## 7.4 Maintaining the Soil-based beds

- It's important to add compost to the beds on a rotating basis. It's also important to add properly conditioned compost. I'll leave it, at this time, to the reader to research and develop a compost technique of their own. The second in this series *" Aquaponics in a Changing World"* will cover, in depth, comprehensive composting techniques.
- Don't churn the soil or disturb it any more than necessary. "Tilling", though a habit of industrial farmers, is not helpful to the soil and does more harm as the bacteria, fungi, micro-fauna and macro-fauna are churned to the surface and killed by the blade, sunlight and lack of moisture. If you want to "loosen" the soil "punch" down through it with a pitch fork and "rock" the fork back and forth.

**Rotating Composters**

- Worms are the farmer's best friend and you need to get some and give them a good home. Worms aerate the soil and provide a loose pack. Their fresh castings are renown for the rich nutrients provided. I leave it to the reader to research and study worms for their own garden in their home environment. The second in the series *"Aquaponics in a Changing World"* visits the fascinating world of vermiculture.

- At CRA we have begun soil *"injection"* research where we burrow into the length of the soil creating a one inch diameter hole - the point of injection - which is then back-filled with additives and covered over. We are using this method to supplement the soil without disturbing it. The example illustrated represents a mix of bone meal, greensand, Azomite and tri-calcium phosphate that boosts plant health, flowering and fruit growth. We will be providing more information and details concerning injection methods in future publications.

*Soil Injection - Selecting the Injection Point*

*Soil Injection - Creating the Injection Point*

*Injecting Plant Nutrients*

*Soil Injection - Backfilling the Injection Point*

- Pests can be controlled with various methods. AzaMax is the pest control choice at CRA. To defeat pests "punch" down through the soil with a pitch fork and follow with a diluted drench of the pest control of your choice. Lightly water to draw the control down into the soil. If the plants can be salvaged use a mist of a diluted pest control on the foliage.

*BE CAREFUL!!! Many pesticides - organically approved or not - can be detrimental to the lives of the fish and any aquaculture. Always visit a product's MSDS (Material Safety Data Sheet) to determine the effects on the fish and aquaculture. In lieu of that DO NOT assume the pesticide used is safe for your fish.*

- Chlorine helps plants control water loss and moisture stress. Though chlorine is found in muriate of potash, manure and greensand it is advised to water the garden occasionally with municipal water as it contains chlorine and will boost the soil content.

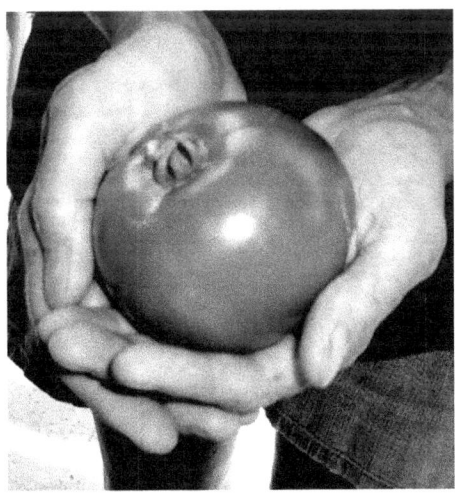

*A GIFT!*

## VIII. Operating the *Aqua-Pod* Garden

With the *Aqua-Pod* constructed, fish and plants in place, bio-filter
cycling and soil-based beds seeded, it's time to discuss the operation
of the garden. Since aquaponics is a year-round operation, the
discussion will focus on two crops per year. Over time this can be
scheduled to achieve a smooth operation of constant seeding,
planting and harvesting where abundance and variety are constantly
available. Interior operations – greenhouses or artificial lighting –
are particularly conducive to achieving this quality method. The
following is assuming one crop planted in October and another in
April. These are Tampa Bay, Florida conditions, but the methods
discussed can be applied to interior operations – both greenhouse
and artificial lighting techniques.

### Daily Items (morning) – 10 minutes

- Feed the fish. Use a good-quality tilapia fish food pellet (or
  that food for whatever species you may be working with). To
  feed the fry, grind the pellets in a coffee grinder or similar
  device. Do not over feed the fish. Feed once per day –
  regardless of what you may have been told – and after 10
  minutes remove excess pellets from the tank surfaces with a
  net. It's cruel and unhealthy to "power" feed fish, and it's
  dirty. At CRA R&D we refuse to purchase and consume any
  farm-raised fish. Fish food can be purchased online for
  reasonable prices, and a ten-pound bag lasts several months
  feeding a single *Aqua-Pod* system with 85 fish of various sizes
  and fry.

- Test the tank/ponds pH with a pH meter. The pH should be
  between 7.0 and 7.6. If the pH is high, dose with a small
  amount (one cup) of distilled white vinegar. If the pH is low,

dose with two tablespoons of baking soda. Do not "chase" pH levels, and when adjusting, dose to achieve a 0.1 change per day. There is a reason the pH is swinging – overpopulation, a compromised bio-filter, inadequate plant filtering, rotting debris, temperature swings. Discover the problem and correct it. When in doubt do a hefty "change-out" – 30 percent - with follow-up pH tests each day. Your nose is a great help – pay attention to odors.

The only time pH has been corrected at CRA R&D was during the initial establishment of the bio-filter on the first unit placed into service.

- Measure TDS (total dissolved solids), using an inexpensive meter. Watch the TDS as a backup indicator with the pH readings. TDS can be a good indicator of overpopulation and rotting debris (plant leaves, excess fish food, a dead fish on the bottom). TDS of municipal source water will be from 170 to 210 ppm. TDS in an active system is between 270 and 320 ppm. Know and follow the TDS to track any wide swings that could indicate problems on the horizon.

- Check water clarity. Using a clear container, draw a sample and hold it up to the light, placing a finger on the opposite side. Rate clarity between 1 and 5, 1 being the best. The sample will have a slight copper-colored hue, but clarity should not be affected. When clarity slips to a 2, proceed with a change-out of 10 to 30 percent and follow-up daily. A continuing loss of clarity can signal a problem that needs to be identified and corrected.

***Check the Water Clarity Daily***

A large array of diagnostic tools is available to assist the operator when questions arise. Oxygen, nitrite, nitrate and ammonia test kits are available at a reasonable cost and at ready access. The titrating compounds in these kits do not have a long shelf life, so buy the smallest kit available. A good aquarium store or the internet is the best source for these test kits. pH test strips are also available, but in the long run they are an expensive proposition. The meters are inexpensive and can be ordered online. Ordering nitrate test strips was a bit problematic for security reasons (we assume because of the creation of fertilizer-based bombs, such as was used in the Oklahoma Federal Building bombing 1995). Still, keep trying and someone will sell them to you. There are a number of electronic probes available, but we have not worked with any of them because they are expensive.

*An Example of Meters and Reagents Available*

*At CRA R&D we have never experienced a bio-filter collapse or had a major loss of aquatic life in 7(+) years of operations. This can be directly attributed to close vigilance and knowledgeable use of the tools previously discussed.*

- Top the sump tanks with water. This amount (three to six gallons) is minimal, and municipal water may be used without the need to treat for chlorine or chloramines.
- Inspect the hose nozzles from the gravity manifold to the grow tubes, and clear any nozzles that are plugged. The nylon attached at the overflow line to the weir helps greatly with keeping the nozzles running clear of obstructions.
- Inspect the vegetation during the ten minutes it takes for the fish to feed. Trim any dead leaves and pick vegetables for the day's consumption.

## Daily items (evening) – 5 minutes

- Top off the systems with water – two to five gallons.

164

- Feed the fish some duckweed. Grow duckweed in the grow tubes or weir sump and dip your hand into the empty sockets and drag off a handful to feed each tank. The fish enjoy it, and it's a good fresh supplement to their diet. CRA R&D obtained at duckweed when we purchased our original blue tilapia fry. It's an aggressive plant, and until your tilapia population matures it is good to skim off the excess from the tanks/ponds surfaces with a net. Observe closely the consumption as the fish mature – there should be no duckweed in the tank/ponds because it's been eaten. Excessive duckweed in the grow tubes can obstruct proper flow cycling and should be maintained by removing for feed or composting.

*The system is topped and properly cycling when the tank/ponds levels are at the designed level where the overflow to the weir tank is constant and the overflow from the weir to the pump sump is also constant. The pump start/stop is triggered by the float switch installed in the sump tank. Take critical note of the tank/pond levels when the cycle is in equilibrium, and carry out "topping" to meet these criteria. The system can be over topped, resulting in tank/pond overflow. It is probably not a critical issue in most installations, but with some operations – those located in high drought areas of the world – the loss of water cannot be tolerated. Following a few attempts the operator will find what works best in a proper "topping" of their Aqua-Pod.*

*Duckweed Growing in Weir Sump*

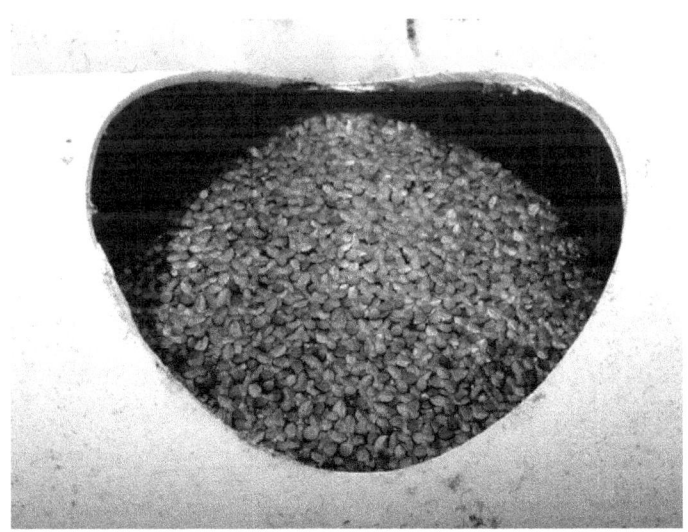

*Duckweed Growth in the Grow Tubes*

## Water "change-outs" and feeding the hybrid soil-based plants – 30 minutes

A 20 percent "change-out" is recommended every four days, or as needed to keep soil at proper moisture levels and feed the plants. To test the soil moisture, insert a finger and determine whether there is any "packing" quality to the soil. If there is none, then a change-out should be done at the first available opportunity. If the *Aqua-Pod* TDS levels reach 320 ppm a change-out is also required.

- If the hose and pump are not already run out, do so now. For expediency keep the pump and hose connected and, where possible, leave the hose and power cord run out.
- Position the hose discharge from the pump at the first soil bed.
- Submerge the pump into the first tank/pond and plug the pump into a 110V properly grounded and GFI-protected power source.
- Split 20 percent of the first tank/pond among four of the grow beds and move the hose to the fifth bed. Lift the running pump out of the first tank and place into the second tank.
- Split 20 percent of the second tank/pond between beds five through eight and move hose to bed nine. Lift the running pump from the tank second to the third tank.
- Split 20 percent of the third tank/pond among beds nine through twelve and secure the pump power.
- Remove the pump from the third tank/pond and lay out the hose and cord for the next use.

*Water change-outs and plant feedings are not an exercise in precision. When a 20 percent change-out is suggested, just shoot for the best percentage possible. Ideally you want to "flood" the beds to the upper edge of the barrel, providing three to five days between change-outs/feedings, depending on heat, humidity and sun intensity. With a properly cycling system it is virtually impossible to compromise the bio-filter cycle. How do you know you have a healthy cycle running? Check your pH, TDS, clarity and odor – daily! Enough effluent remains in the tubes to jump start the system even following a full evacuation of the tank/ponds during the annual "clean and count" event.*

Change-out is a good time to harvest fish for consumption. The tank level is reduced and the tilapia are easier to net and remove. Tilapia are active, feisty fish and not at all docile when it comes to being captured. The lower the water levels the easier they are to corral and capture.

*2014, in the Tampa Bay area, was the hottest and driest since CRA R&D began operations in early 2009 (global warming?). We have used more system effluent in the beds than ever before. It hasn't posed a problem outside of a 2 percent increase in consumption of municipal water. Even taking the increase into consideration we use – at most – 6 percent of the water required in industrial agriculture and we get our vegetation fed nitrates with it!*

## Weekly items – 1 to 4 hours

- Renew the nylon filter at the overflow return line to the weir if necessary. Dry the old filter and then cut it open and add the rich fertilizer to the composter.
- Feed the composter with the weekly house waste, and manually fork or rotate unit.
- Weed the soil beds.

- Clear all plants of dead leaves in both the *Aqua-Pod* and soil beds. Inspect for invasive bugs and remove them. If necessary, remove plants from the *Aqua-Pod* and spray – away from tanks/ponds – with AzaMax. Replace plants after three hours. Spray hybrid soil-based plants downwind of tanks/ponds.
- Remove any depleted plants from the *Aqua-Pod* and soil beds and compost. Renew the net pot medium with cleaned, dry pellets. Prep the soil for replanting. Replant as needed.
- Assess the vegetation and start seed to fill in future areas as plants mature and fade out.
- Remove or separate seed to dry for future use.
- Bag, tag and refrigerate dried seed for future use.
- Add potassium, calcium, magnesium and iron to the *Aqua-Pod* weir tank.

*It is important to be seeding constantly. With 216 grow-tube sockets, there is room to bring plants to maturity in either the Aqua-Pod or in the soil beds. As previously discussed, it is inexpensive when reclaiming seed from current plant stock. It's also good to keep an eye out for vegetables that can be purchased, tasted and – if to your liking – seeded and grown. Most communities have seed/plant exchanges where seed/plants can be swapped along with suggestions and advice. Your county agriculture extension office is a good source in providing plant and planting guidelines and information on pests, weather conditions and water quality. Be aware that the extension office is primarily involved with supplying information to industrial farmers and the methods industrial farming uses. Plants that the extension office suggests can be grown are not the only ones that can be grown. Because of the ease and positive returns with the Aqua-Pod it's good to branch out and experiment. Not everything will work (you'll be surprised at how much does succeed!) but attempting and succeeding is the most satisfying return. Planning and implementing a plan are a good weekly task to pursue.*

## Monthly items – 1 ½ hours

• Trim the roots of *Aqua-Pod* plants by removing and cutting back to the net with shears or a sharp knife. Place the removed roots in the composter system. Roots can also be fed to the fish or poultry on the farm.

*Plant Roots are Trimmed Monthly*

170

-     This is the time to get a close look at the plants. Basket-grown aquaponics give the operator insight that no other method can. Hold the plant basket in your hand at or above eye level. Observe the leaf structure and any imperfections. These observations may lead to decisions or changes about seed to be stocked and re-grown. Like any grower, you must make your best attempts to achieve a hearty, tasty plant. Use the internet to research any insects and larva you find. The vast majority of insects and spiders are helpful for growth and protection against harmful invaders. Butterfly caterpillars can consume a lot of vegetation but should, if possible, be left alone. If you want, you can move the caterpillars to a central "sacrificial" plant where they can mature, cocoon and survive. Butterflies, like many helpful insects, including honey bees, are having a tough time with the Big Ag "advances" like Roundup, and they now depend on the organic farmer to survive. Be prepared to come eye to eye with a praying mantis – this beautiful creatures is so well camouflaged that you must be, literally, eye to eye before you can see it.

*Monarch Butterfly Larva on Parsley*

- Back-flush the tank/ponds return piping to the weir with a hose and nozzle to keep it clean them and clear.

Monthly items can be incorporated into weekly chores, or they can be spread out over time. You can develop your own routine of daily, weekly and monthly items. Always keep in mind the importance of maintaining the bio-filter in growing fat, happy and healthy fish and harvesting good vegetables and fruits.

## Semi-annually

This discussion focuses on seeding and planting. Maintenance of a healthy bio-filer and adequate vegetative growth is of the greatest importance in maintaining the cycle by taking up the nitrates produced. Greenhouse or artificial lighting techniques do not pose any challenges to harvesting, seeding and planting, as these can be done throughout the year. Greenhouse installations will – for the most part – generate more robust growth during the seasons with longer days, but the fall and winter sunlight periods will not jeopardize a functioning bio-filter cycle. Exterior operations are another matter, depending on local conditions. Heightened temperature and humidity – such as we have at the CRA – can make growing a number of plants difficult during the summer months. Operations in climates with monsoon seasons need to plant appropriately for harsh wet conditions, thus maintaining a properly cycling bio-filter.

At the beginning of operations plan a crop schedule by understanding what is suitable to your specific locale. A good place to start is the local agriculture extension office, online, at the library, or you can visit their offices. Frequent local farmers' markets to discover what is being produced locally (a great source of seed).

- Establish semi-annual dates, and research plants to seed and grow. In the Tampa Bay area of Florida, the growing seasons start in October and April. October follows the heat of summer, while April is the start of summer. In both instances young plants aren't subjected to crushing conditions of high heat and humidity (September) or overnight cools (March).
- Obtain sufficient quantities of seed.
- Start seedlings and, if transferring to the soil, plant when sprouts are strong and healthy.

Some plants can be grown year round – tomatoes, beans, celery, lettuces, beets to name a few – and some plants are cold averse or heat averse. The Brussels sprout is an example of a heat-averse plant, while succulents – such as Cuban oregano and aloe – do not tolerate frosts. Plants averse to frost are best removed from the grow tubes, the roots trimmed to the basket nets and stored inside for the night. I'll repeat the most important point of this discussion – *do not compromise your bio-filter!*

## Annual Clean and Count – 3 hours

It's good to keep track of the fish production, and this is best achieved by removing the fish to an alternate holding tank and counting them. With the fish removed, evacuate the tanks/ponds for inspection and cleaning.

- Prepare a holding tank to transfer the fish temporarily. Dechlorinate the holding tank and fill it with fresh water. Check the temperature of the water; if it is too cool, wait for it to warm in the sunlight before transferring the fish. CRA R&D uses a 55-gallon aquarium, allowing us to closely observe the fish. Tilapias are mouth breeders. The aquarium permits observance of this phenomena and it also permits a close look at any marks or scars on the fish

*Inspecting the Fish in a "Holding" Aquarium*

- It's important to save off 50 gallons of tanks/ponds water for healthy bio-filter maintenance when re-starting the cleaned system. Set up a barrel with the lid removed or a sufficient hole cut into the lid to permit a submersible pump to be placed at the barrel bottom. When the barrel is full transfer the remaining effluent to the soil beds.
- Submerge the pump into the first tank/pond and start pumping water into the barrel as instructed in the previous step. With a net, begin removing tilapia to the holding tank. Tilapia are tough, feisty fish and difficult to capture. Be prepared to take the tank/pond to a minimal level before you will be able to get all the fish out. As the level reaches to two to three inches, closely watch for any fry. If fry are evident stop pumping and remove as many as possible with a fine mesh net and keep in a five-gallon bucket with de-chlorinated water.
- With fish and fry removed, pump the tank/pond empty.
- Repeat the steps with the remaining tank/ponds.
- It isn't possible to remove all the water with the submersible pump. Employ a wet/dry vacuum if necessary. There should not be much, if any, dirt/slime buildup, and you may find no need to proceed further. At CRA R&D we choose

to give the tank/ponds a good hosing down while paying close attention to the conditions we find. We then vacuum the remaining water and hand wipe the tank/ponds.

*Do not use a detergent or soap to clean tank/ponds. The "slime" on the surfaces is actually the bio-filter, and cleaning it with soaps or detergents will destroy it and may destroy the system bio-filter. Hand wiping is okay because, unless you wait several days and the tank/ponds fully dry, there is plenty of slime still adhering to the tank/ponds surfaces.*

- Backfill one tank/pond with the saved off water by submerging the pump in the barrel.
- Treat the tanks/ponds with de-chlorinator and fill from the municipal supply. Check the temperature and if the water is too cool wait until the temperature stabilizes and matches water temperature of 55-gallon holding aquarium.
- Replace the fish to the tank/ponds by size. Put eight-inch and larger fish to an outside tank, four- to eight-inch fish into the other outside tank, and fry to four-inch fish in the middle tank. Count the fish going into each tank and record for comparison each year. The largest fish are placed to the outside tanks/ponds because these are going to be harvested, and the outside tanks provide the easiest access.
- Restart the system and top up the system for proper operation.

The grow tubes hold sufficient fluids to prevent the loss of the bio-filter after a clean and count period, but we have experienced a slowing of plant growth for two or three weeks when we don't save off a barrel (50 gallons) of water from the each *Aqua-Pod* system. The fry are nearly impossible to count. At CRA R&D we estimated that 1,000 to 1500 fry were present at last "clean and count," and each *Aqua-Pod* unit averaged 85 fish between 1 inch and 17 inches in size. Tilapia, like most fish, is able to discern the conditions of their environment and maintain a population level to meet that environment. They control the population density by eating their young.

*Aquaponics is a labor of love of plants and aquatic life, and the decision to enter the business should not be taken lightly. If you don't like groveling in the dirt, seeding and weeding, and working with fish – and all that requires – don't get involved with the science. Like all farming, aquaponics requires a commitment of blood, sweat and tears. And, like all farming, it returns rewards well worth the sacrifice.*

## Estimated Monthly Operating Costs

### Electrical costs/month @ $0 .057 per kWh:

- Sump pump – 12 hours run time/day, one unit @ 127 watts = $5.33/month
- Aerators – 24 hours/day usage, three units @ 2.9 watts = $0.48/month
- Heater – 12 hours/day, three units @ 400 watts = $33.60/month

It can be tough to estimate heater costs as it depends on the severity of any temperature drop. The heaters are set to maintain water temperatures of 65°F. The 2013–2014 winter season required the operation of submerged heaters for 15 days. The 2009–2010 season required heater operation for 37 days. The *Aqua-Pod* skirt/aprons greatly reduce wind shear to the tank/ponds. Wind shear has a much greater effect on temperature than a simple drop in ambient temperature. With 450 gallons of water you can maintain a temperature very well for an extended period, and if the days are warm little energy is used to meet a 65°F demand as the cold late night/early morning progresses. Long spells of cool temperatures – day in and day out – can turn the hobbyist into seasoned farmer in a very short period of time.

## Fish Feed Costs

CRA R&D is located in a part of the world where large amounts of fresh water ornamental fish are raised. With that in mind, we are able to buy bulk at wholesale prices. Quality fish food can be ordered on the internet. CRA R&D uses approximately two pounds of feed per month per unit. CRA R&D also grows and feeds duckweed to the fish daily - $5.00

## Chlorine/chloramines treatment costs

A gallon for $55 lasts over a year when compounding five units every three or four days - $4.00

Added minerals costs: These are very inexpensive additives and are a minor cost factor - $2.00

**Labor:** The bare minimum is 6.5 hours/month. That covers only routine daily to annual tasks as listed previously and does not include time spent on the following:

- selecting, acquiring and seeding plants.
- repairs or increasing operation size and capacity.
- researching or travel to acquire necessities or visits to other aquaponic operations.

- maintaining communications within the sustainable farming community.

*Operating an aquaponic farm is like anything else in life – you get out of it what you put into it. Remember that the health of the bio-filter and the health of the aquaculture take precedence in all situations. Operating any farm with animals is a long-term commitment and involves hard work. If working with fish and plants – and all that it involves – is not a passion, then please do yourself and the fish a favor: Find another way to contribute to the sustainable community. If you do have a passion for this discipline, please become involved. We're behind the curve on this technology, and humanity needs all the help it can get.*

## IX. Plant Selection and Seeding

**_Flowering Okra Plant_**

The testing and subsequent growing of plants in a new prototype system like the *Aqua-Pod* can be a rewarding yet humbling task. The simple reality is one cannot make things happen any faster than nature is going to let things happen – it takes time and it takes patience. Here in the Tampa Bay area we are lucky because we can grow all year. That doesn't mean we can grow all crops all year round, and there are some plants we have difficulty growing at any time of the year. Some plants do better in the *Aqua-Pod*s and some do better in the soil. This is main focus of our research – what plants do best, where and when.

There are two windows of the year when we plan and install our plants – October and April. That requires seeding of plants in September and March. The October planting selection offers the widest variety due to the cooler months; the April planting selection is more limited due to the heat of summer, but harvests are more abundant.

Interior operations with the *Aqua-Pod* and farm/garden permit year-round growing opportunities without constraints due to ambient weather conditions but for a healthy bio-filter it remains important that a disciplined planting and growing schedule be established and followed. Most, if not all, of the plants discussed here can be grown in greenhouses or under artificial lighting. In reality, interior operations are limited only by taste, seed/plant acquisition and the farmer's imagination.

The plants discussed here reflect the CRA exterior conditions. If you are operating interior spaces, you can disregard remarks about seasonal conditions. I'll spend little time discussing scientific names for the plants; instead, I'll use generic descriptions. The success of each plant will be rated. I'll open with the plants we have the greatest problems with.

**Melons, Squashes and Cucumbers** give us the greatest problems. Aphids and leaf miners wreak havoc on these plants, and though we get fruit, it is often unable to mature before the leafy vegetation is devoured. We do achieve fruit maturity by spraying AzaMax – but it is quite costly and it can be toxic to the fish. We take some fruits and vegetables to maximum maturity and then save the seed, hoping that as we re-seed each season a stronger, more pest-resistant plant will develop. Currently we are experiencing success with multi-generation seeds of watermelons, cucumbers and zucchini. We have recently begun to work with insecticidal soaps with varying success. Our research in this area is limited and, at his time, we cannot make any specific recommendations. A number of concoctions – all organic – are available and can be researched on the internet.

*Watermelon*

*Flowering Zucchini*

### *Aqua-Pod* and Hybrid Soil-based Vegetation

- **Cuban oregano**– one of the system "workhorses," is propagated with cuttings. It is a hardy plant that requires root and plant trimming on a monthly basis. It is not grown in the soil beds.

*The term "workhorse" describes a plant with good "take-up" qualities as pertains to the Aqua-Pod. A "workhorse" can take up ammonia, nitrites and nitrates and is particularly beneficial during bio-filter establishment and for bio-filter maintenance. The plants can be added to the Aqua-Pod as fish population gains in number and weight, and they can be removed with a decrease in fish (harvesting) or with increases in other plants in the system.*

- **Celery**– is another system workhorse. We do not grow celery in the soil beds because it grows much faster in the *Aqua-Pod*.

*Celery and Cuban Oregano*

- **Aloe**– another system workhorse, is propagated with cuttings. Aloe is also grown in very limited quantities in soil-based "planters" for medicinal use.
- **Parsley** – curly and flat leaf – is grown year round in the systems as opposed to only the October planting in soil-based beds.

*Curly Leaf Parsley*

- **Cherry "Bush" Tomatoes** – are trimmed to keep bush shape in the systems and grown year-round in soil beds. There is a large variety of "cherries" available providing for different tastes and textures.

*Purple Cherry Tomatoes*

- **Bok Choy** is grown in both the systems and in the soil beds.
- **Swiss Chard** like bok choy, is grown in both the systems and the soil beds.

*Swiss Chard*

- **Roma Tomatoes–** do well when they are placed at the system edges. The plant will grow down (upside down), with an excellent crop. We tend to keep the roma's in the systems leaving room in the soil beds for other tomato varieties.
- **Avocado–** the platform is great starter for avocados seeds. Transfer the plant to soil at 10" height and with 3(+) leaves.

*Hybrid soil-based beds are an integral part of the Aqua-Pod farm/garden for several reasons. They significantly increase variety and returns with a minimal increase in water usage. With soil-based operations, plants are grown using less than 6 percent of the water that industrial farming requires. Feeding/watering soil-based plants greatly enhances the maintenance of a healthy bio-filter, with fluctuating conditions of the Aqua-Pod – increasing/decreasing fish populations/weights and increasing/decreasing system plant numbers and maturity.*

- **Pineapples–** a recent addition to the systems and very promising – another workhorse. We grow pineapples in the native soil here in Florida.
- **Shallots–** have a much shorter growing period in the *Aqua-Pod* compared to soil-based growth. We do "break" the shallots up and, when inundated with them, re-plant them into the soil beds.

*Shallots and Flowers*

- **Onions**– like shallots, are grown in both the systems and the soil-based beds.
- **Beets**– are grown in the systems only. The increased rate of growth, when compared with soil-based growth, is such as to negate the use in soil-based operations.

*Beets and Flowers*

- **Scallions–** are "seeded" in the systems and them broken up and planted in the soil-based beds.
- **Basil–** all types do very well in the systems with accelerated growth. Because of this we grow some in the soil-based beds for daily food "seasoning" and use the system "crop" to make several varieties of "pesto" twice a year to freeze.

*Baby Purple Basil*

- **Cilantro–** is trimmed to maintain lush foliage. It is best to start the cilantro in the system and then move it to the soil-based beds. This permits the room to grow the plant out to "seed" so it can be collected, dried and used as coriander.
- **Dill–** is trimmed to maintain a lush foliage. Dill grows well in both the systems and the soil.

*Dill*

- **Asian Peppers** can be grown with either methods.

*To grow peppers in the system, like many vegetables, the plants are trimmed back and managed. This produces more flowers and fruit in a limited space. It's best to start larger peppers in the systems and then re-plant to the soil-based beds.*

*Purple Bell Peppers*

*Orange Bell Peppers*

- Bell Peppers.
- Poblano Peppers.
- Anaheim Peppers.

*Anaheim Peppers*

- Banana Peppers.
- Jalapeño Peppers

*Jalapeño Peppers*

- **Okra**– is a very successful plant that offers plant shading during the hot summer season. Grow some in the systems to protect young growth in the heat of summer. The majority grown at CRA is in soil-based beds.

*Okra*

- **Marigolds**– are used for pest control in both the systems and the soil-based beds.
- **Lettuces**– all lettuces do well in the *Aqua-Pod* with the exception of iceberg – it doesn't ball. Lettuce is a "no brainer" in aquaponics... seed it and it grows. At CRA we have grown dozens of types with great results. The problem with lettuce is consuming the quantities grown.

*Lettuce - a "No Brainer" in the Aqua-Pod*

*More Lettuce*

### *and... More Lettuce!*

- **Kale-** is grown in the systems and the soil-based beds with excellent returns. At CRA we have moved towards a greater production of kale while reducing out-put production of lettuces to meet our taste preferences - we grow mostly romaine, arugula, endive and butter-head varieties of lettuce.

*Kale*

- **Carrots**- are seeded in the systems and then transferred to the soil-based beds.
- **Broccoli**– offers good returns in October planting with fair results with April planting. It is grown year round, but in hot weather the florets need to be picked smaller and more often or they go to flower.
- **Tomatoes**– offer excellent returns, a wide variety are grown year round.

*Tomatoes on the Vine*

*More Tomatoes*

- **Beans**– excellent returns. Green pole, purple, yard long.

*Green Beans*

*Large tomatoes and green beans are examples of cumbersome plants difficult to work with, and grow, in the confines of the Aqua-Pod. Hence, with these types of plants, unless doing research, they are best seeded in the systems and then re-planted in the soil-based beds. These methods provide for the greatest returns per season "cycle".*

- **Cauliflower**– good returns, grown in soil-based beds only. CRA R&D is situated several miles south of a MOSAIC fertilizer plant. If there are extensive winds from the north, the cauliflower balls get a grayish to black coloring unless covered (imagine what it does to people, pets and wildlife!).
- **Brussels sprouts**– excellent returns, grown in soil-based beds only. October season only - grow Brussels sprouts in the hot season and they don't ball up.

*Budding Brussels Sprouts*

- **Cabbage**– excellent returns, grown in soil-based beds only.

*Cabbage*

- **Kohlrabi**– excellent returns in both the systems and soil-based beds.
- **Egg plants**– excellent returns, grown in soil-based beds only.

*Eggplant*

- **Spinach**– good returns but best in soil-based beds, October planting is better.
- **Radishes-** excellent growth in the systems.

*Radish Grown in the Aqua-Pod*

- **Horse Radish-** return analysis pending, grown in soil-based beds.

*Horse Radish*

- **Sunflowers**– excellent returns, grown in soil-based beds only.
- **Leeks**– excellent returns when grown in both the systems and soil-based beds.

*A Leek Plant*

- **Collards**– excellent returns, grown in soil-based beds.
- **Rhubarb**– excellent returns, grown in native soils and soil-based beds. October planting only.

*I've made references to Aqua-Pod plants growing at increased rates compared to soil-based plants. It is our conclusion that this because the plants are removed from the systems monthly and the roots trimmed back to the net basket and replaced and also because many plants do well in the constant water "bath" of the Aqua-Pod system grow tubes.*

- **Herbs and Spices** – good to excellent returns: thyme, basil, sage, rosemary, Italian oregano, marjoram, fennel, dill, tarragon, cilantro, parsley (October crop only), chives, mint and spearmint.

*Green Chives*

*Sweet Mint*

*Rosemary*

*Marjoram*

*Oregano*

*Sage*

*Herbs and spices are a great place to start when initially planting your garden. They are easy to establish and grow, and the cost savings can be felt within months. Fresh herbs and spices enhance any meal and are fun to give away as gifts during the holidays and special occasions. Take the opportunity to visit your nearest "grocer" and price your favorite herbs... you will be glad you are growing "your own"!*

- Ornamental flowers – marigolds, carnations, dahlia and zinnias. Because our focus in this manual is on the greatest nutritional return, ornamental flower growth will remain limited to this short reference.

*Flowers*

*The weather can be great, the plant stock the best and conditions perfect, but if pests are permitted free rein they'll eat you up.*

## GET OUT AND LOOK AT YOUR PLANTS!

*Eliminate pests manually and use AzaMax as needed. Keep an eye out for lady bugs, frogs, spiders and praying mantises – they will help greatly in reducing harmful pests.*

## Seed and Plant Acquisition

- Acquiring plant stock can be accomplished by purchasing seed and plants from a box store, nursery or seed catalog, by collecting seeds and drying for use from produce grown or bought or by propagating with cuttings from existing plants. Any plants brought in from the outside can also bring in pests – be aware! When in doubt spray the plant(s) with AzaMax to keep pests away from the farm and the soil.

- As previously mentioned – the major focus of the CRA R&D program has been, and remains, the development of the plant & vegetation growth. It's important we know and understand what can be grown with the NFT concept & renewable methods. Though the commercial viability of aquaponics remains, at this time, a topic of debate - as water becomes scarcer; as regulatory bodies enact & enforce laws to contain harmful industrial GMO's, fertilizers, pesticides and herbicides; as fossil fuels become more expensive and as communities commit to greater control of their food sourcing (and the related costs) the NFT concept, and all aquaponics, will become commercially viable as demand increases. With this in mind it is important we continue to work with aquaponics - to research new plants to determine the returns - and develop guidelines to meet current & future demand.

## Seed Collection and Storage

- Harvesting – Plant harvesting is perhaps the most rewarding aspect of growing any food in any manner. Harvesting a food grown in a sustainable manner with the least impact to the Earth and its environs is that much more fulfilling. It's important to let some of the plants of each variety go to flower so the seed can be collected. When a plant life has played itself out and seed has been collected – dry it in the sun and chop it up for compost.

- Collecting your own seed for later use is economical and increases control of the crops grown. Of greater importance is that it provides a bank of seeds that haven't been genetically altered (GMO) by one of the large seed producers. In the USA it's got to the point where a seed buyer doesn't really know whether the seed has been altered, because there are no rules concerning labeling of genetically modified seed (as is required in European Union and many nations). Though the reuse of GMO seed is strictly prohibited by the big seed producers, cross-pollination with adjoining non-GMO fields is a fact, and the seed can be affected. It's also important to save seeds in the hopes that they will, over generations, develop into a more hearty organic strain better able to resist pests and adverse weather conditions with a richer flavor and a stronger fiber.

- Big Ag and industrial seed producers would like us to believe the life span of a plant is 3 to 6 months. That is not true. Tomatoes can go for up to a year, lettuce can go for months in excess of the industrially grown harvest time if a few leaves are picked at a time. Most herbs and spices last indefinitely only requiring they be cut back and thinned occasionally. What we have been told and the methods followed in the industrial sector – both seed/plant supply and plant production – are myths perpetrated to provide the commercial industry, Big Ag and wholesale/retail suppliers with comfortable profits all while the Earth is slowly strangled by the excessive use of fossil fuels, industrial fertilizers, pesticides and herbicides that are killing the pollinators and destroying the water and air.

- Biennial seeds – Many plants – cabbages, beets, celery, onions and carrots, to name a few – are biennial. This means they take two growing seasons – with a frost or two in between – to reach the stage where flowering occurs; followed by the death of the plant. Growing outdoors in the Tampa Bay area provides the climate and conditions needed to flower and collect biennial seed (usually). As with exterior operations, where a frost may not occur, interior operations with the *Aqua-Pod* requires some planning to achieve the "frost" conditions required to drive the biennial plant into the flowering stage. CRA R&D has experimented by removing the plant from the system, cutting the roots back to the basket, placing the plant in a freezer for 10 to 30 minutes and then replacing it in the *Aqua-Pod*. Thus the "biennial" is not actually a two-year period; rather it's one season plus a good frost following the first plant maturity. "Ambient" conditions can be used by placing the plant outside during a frost for a short period of time in the same manner as placing it in a freezer. For both the farmer in climates with little to no frosts and the interior operator; your biennials will require some creative measures to ensure the acquisition of seed.

- Annuals seeds – Annuals are left to flower and the seed is collected and dried.
- Seed drying– Dry the seeds on newspaper (one that uses soy-based ink) or on aluminum foil for about a week. A properly dried seed will not stick to the newspaper or foil and can be easily separated from other seeds and moved about using a wooden stick. Try not to handle the seed with your hands. Seed pods can be left to dry and the entire pod stored and then opened at planting.
- Seed storage – Store the seed in airtight containers – plastic bags or glass or plastic jars and containers. Date the seed, and don't use older seed unless necessary. Most seed is good for two to three years. Store the seed in a refrigerator, as far from the freezer section as possible. Remove the seed and let it come to ambient temperature before opening. This prevents moisture from causing the seed to clump, making it difficult to handle.
- Collecting, storing and replanting seed is an empowering task. It greatly enhances the financial bottom line; the grower is comfortable knowing exactly where the seed came from and its history; the seed is not a GMO; and, a storage bank of seed is created, available and at hand when needed.

### A Final Note:

*I've taken a good bit of my time, and I'm sure the reader's time, to document throughout this manual, and in this section in particular, plants tested, developed and grown at the CRA location using the Aqua-Pod as the central component. I do this to give the reader an idea of the unlimited potential of aquaponics to grow proteins and edible plants that have every potential of feeding the human inhabitants of this world we call "home".*

## *NO PLANT GROWN AND EXHIBITED HEREIN HAS REQUIRED ANY SYNTHETIC FERTILIZERS, PESTICIDES OR HEBICIDES - NOT ONE!*

### *Furthermore:*

*Upon venturing out into the "aquaponics community" one can find numerous "offerings" for incredible amounts in investment dollars that are "guaranteed" to make you a "wealthy" aquaponic "operator" by producing "X" numbers of heads of lettuce per week/month/year. These "unassembled" aquaponics operations can cost from hundreds to several hundreds of thousands of dollars. Once purchased you're pretty much on your own unless, of coarse, you want to sink a few more thousands into the "schools" the unit sellers operate. Hey... I have nothing against someone making an honest dollar but it's disingenuous to "hood wink" a person into believing they can make a living selling little heads of lettuce in the community. Furthermore... it leaves people with a bad taste in their mouths when they consider the field of "aquaponics".*

## *AQUAPONICS WILL ACHIEVE TRACTION WHEN PEOPLE UNDERSTAND THEY CAN GROW - AND CONTROL – A VARIETY OF REAL FOOD THAT CAN BE EATEN DAILY AND ENJOYED.*

# X. Growing from Garden to Farm

*When Cyrson Ranch Aquaponics Research and Development began operations in 2008, it was our opinion that due to changing climate conditions and dwindling fuel and water supplies, aquaponics would take a firm hold providing vegetables and protein for human consumption in 50 to 75 years. Current conditions and continuing studies over the past seven years have led us to believe that aquaponics will assume a major role in 15 to 25 years. Our farm, by no means the size needed for a commercial operation, is laid out in a manner that offers a glimpse at what a commercial operation can be when expanded. It is also our intention to provide for the development of urban community farming, which we believe will play a major role in future protein and vegetable production.*

*If you are interested in growing your operation, this offers the best place to start.*

## CRA R&D General Component description

- Five *Aqua-Pod* units are constructed, with fourteen 150-gallon tanks/ponds holding a total of 2100 gallons of water.
- Each *Aqua-Pod* holds 12 grow tubes, averaging 216 net pot sockets and providing approximately 900 sockets for plant growth.
- Each *Aqua-Pod* has its own circulation system – pump, distribution manifold, tank return pipes, overflow weir and pump sump.

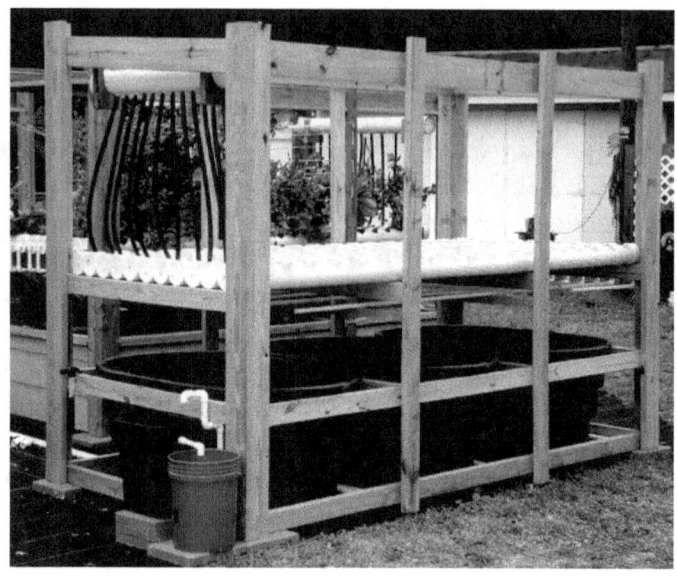

*The Aqua-Pod with Tanks, Grow Tubes and Recirculation Systems Installed*

- There are 64 soil-based planters.

*Soil-Based Planters*

- There are two 275-gallon holding tanks for treating municipal water and storing water/effluent.

*Tanks for Storage and Water Treatment*

- A centrally located 720-gallon-per-hour transfer pump is used to evacuate the systems, feed/water soil-based grow beds and to refill the tank/ponds.

*Farm Transfer Pump*

- PVC piping is installed from the municipal water source to each *Aqua-Pod* sump and the treating and storage tanks; it can be crossed over to the soil-based feed/watering system.
- The transfer pump takes suction from the desired *Aqua-Pod* and the feed/water is distributed to one of 8 "bundled" soil-based (8 per bundle) beds through installed piping and valves.
- There is a 200' reeled hose for feeding/watering citrus trees, a banana tree, avocado trees and a number of ornamentals.

***200' Hose Reeled***

- Tank/ponds are backfilled using the hose with the transfer pump suction from the treatment/storage tanks.
- When the tanks/ponds are evacuated (yearly) one storage treatment tank is filled, using the transfer pump, and then the water is returned to the systems to ensure a quality bio-filter on restarting the systems.

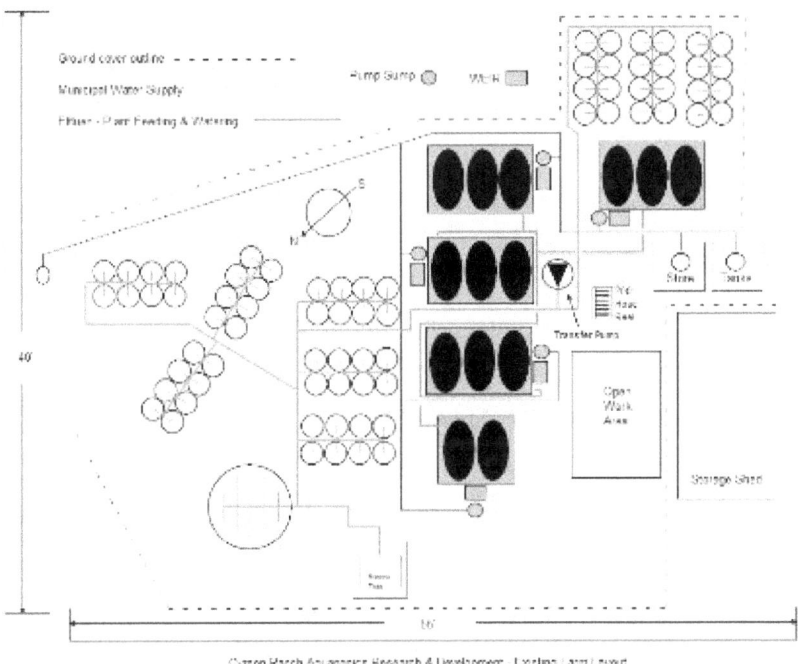

*Farm Layout - Cyrson Ranch Aquaponics Research and Development*

## Design, Construction and Operation of an Aquaponic Farm with the *Aqua-Pod* Platform

As you might expect, the Cyrson Ranch Aquaponics R & D system did not come together in one shot. We made alterations throughout the construction of the first three units until we were satisfied that we had a good platform offering the greatest nutritional value per square foot area used. The first three units have names – Pee Wee , Rosa Parks , and Big Boy. Though it may sound cute that these units are named (as concerns Rosa Parks it was a matter of respect) there is a method to our madness. With constant ongoing discussions of each unit (along with an argument or three) – design tweaks, positives, negatives, returns in production, ease of operation and costs – it was easier refer to units by name. The final two units – #4 and #5 – are cookie-cutter builds developed from the knowledge gained in the development of Pee Wee, Rosa and Big Boy. It will become evident that Rosa, Big Boy, #4 and #5 are essentially the same unit and dubbed the *Aqua-Pod*. Pee Wee is a hybrid and the first unit I will discuss.

In December 2008 the Gaza strip was under attack. Listening to reports, realizing the hazards, blockades and checkpoints – and having begun our research in aquaponic growing techniques – we determined we would construct a unit for operation in areas where farmer/family/community movement is restricted while additionally coping with intermittent water and power supplies.

> **"People need a food source close to home. They need a food source that doesn't require traveling through checkpoints, navigating barriers or encountering hazards such as battle zones and mine fields. The food must be grown with a minimum amount of water where water is not always safely or readily available".**

> *Jim Gibson – Designer & Plant Manager, Cyrson Ranch Aquaponic R&D*

Construction of Pee Wee began in March 2009. Pee Wee is a two-tank/ponds unit; 300 gallons of water, using schedule 40 PVC pipes for grow tubes in 4" and 6" diameters. Water is distributed to the tubes in the same manner as the *Aqua-Pod* (as are tank/ponds overflows, weir tank and sump tank designs). Pee Wee differs from the *Aqua-Pod* design in that the grow-tube circulation returns to the tanks/ponds are achieved with holes drilled in the sides of grow tube whereas the *Aqua-Pod* tank/pond returns are routed through pipes installed at the flow end of the 12 grow tubes and equally returned to each of the three tanks/ponds. Pee Wee is designed so that components – grow tubes, distribution manifold and weir tank – are prepared prior to shipping. The frame components are sized, pre-cut and prepped for assembly in the field. Pee Wee's contents are designed to be delivered by crate, light enough for four people to lift and maneuver, and to be transported by animal cart or a flatbed vehicle to the construction location.

Pee Wee was a challenge from the beginning. The grow tubes were positioned too low above the tank/ponds, and to get into a position to observe and/or work with the fish and in the tanks you had to turn your head – very confining and uncomfortable. Aiming to fulfill our mission statement – *"zero tolerance of senseless death of the aquaculture"* – we over-designed the climate control, with excessive costs for water cooling (a 1 HP chiller) and insulation against the cold (custom clear exterior covers). The electrical supply was too complicated, as was the top covering. Other than these problems, Pee Wee proved the basic concept viable and productive.

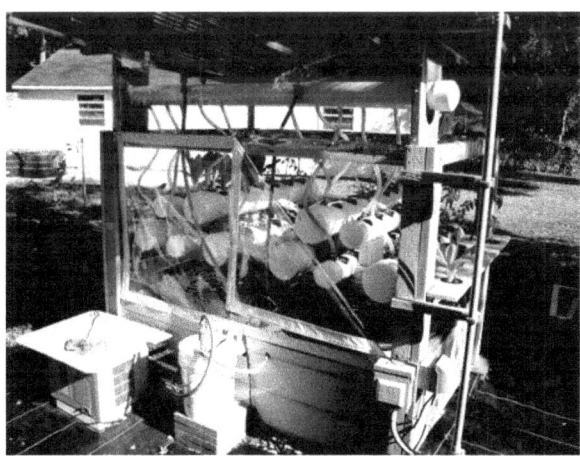

*"Pee Wee" - 2 Tanks, Water Chiller and an Electrical Nightmare*

*"Pee Wee" - A Closer Look*

Pee Wee was placed into service in April 2009 and began with 100 purchased feeder fish producing lettuce. Four weeks later the water was green and had a pungent odor, and pH had risen to 8.9. It was then decided we would "condition" the pH with distilled white vinegar. Following daily additions of vinegar at half a cup per day, the pH was 7.0, clarity was excellent, the odor was gone and the system was *"cycling"*. The bio-filter was balanced and the system was producing. At this time it was decided to leave Pee Wee "as is" and move on with the development of another, bigger and better, unit.

The design approach to the second unit – Rosa Parks – was to correct existing problems and bring construction costs down. The heavy-schedule 4" and 6" PVC we had previously used was expensive; we decided to use solid drain pipe of a lighter schedule and lower cost. This pipe comes in 10 ½' lengths with ½' belled ends to permit connecting consecutive pipes for any length required. For use in the *Aqua-Pod*, the bell end is removed, leaving a 10' run. It became obvious that with a properly framed unit using the lighter-schedule 10' grow pipes, a three-tank/pond system could be constructed, offering significant savings with a one third increase in production of vegetation and proteins.

*In November of 2009 a two-year technical data collection discipline established. Technical data included temperatures; ambient high/low, tanks, chiller, laboratory tanks, chemistry; pH, TDS, clarity, ammonia, nitrates, nitrites [ammonia, nitrates and nitrites were discontinued early in the testing program], vegetation; growth rates, appearance and taste, fish; growth rates and deaths, rainfall and water added to system pump sumps. As we still do, we kept notes of all plants grown, or attempted to be grown, any fish taken for food, and miscellaneous items of note.*

*In addition, for the first two years – until the conclusion of data collection – all fish used in the system were sampled and grown in laboratory conditions, permitting easy inspection and analysis concerning proper feeding, any health issues and to assist in calculating birth and growth rates. After the two-year period, the lab was dismantled and all non-tilapia fish were given away or added to several ornamental aquariums in the home at CRA R&D.*

*Some might argue that this data collection and research was not required. It is our judgment that to build an intimate knowledge of the process – and in return gain the confidence to continue and grow – familiarization was essential.*

Rosa was constructed and placed in service in April 2010 with African cichlids and blue tilapia with one hundred tilapia "fry" acquired through Craig's List.

Rosa Parks is a 100-percent screwed construction. When the same grow-pipe overflow technique used on Pee Wee was tested (holes drilled at half the diameter height in the grow tubes) we found that too much water was lost between the tanks as it rained back down and into the tanks. To correct this, the end caps opposite the gravity manifold were drilled out to accommodate a ½" NPT tapped EL, and ½" PVC pipe was adapted to take the water away and re-distribute the returns equally to each tank/pond.

*"Rose Parks" - Prior to Commissioning*

Rosa performed well beyond expectations and was initially planted with purple basil. The crop was excellent, and to this day we have frozen pesto even after giving away copious amounts. With the successful construction and operation of Rosa Parks the *Aqua-Pod* was born.

By this time enough data had been collected to project the timing of required water change-outs to maintain a proper bio-filter cycle balance; following extensive discussions, the question arose: *Should we increase the aquaponic vegetation base or should we use the nutrients in a hybrid soil-based, aquaponics-fed system?*

The final answer came to us upon review of our initial mission statement addressing the Pee Wee design. It is our contention that the *"systems provide the greatest amount nutritional value with the least footprint and be able to supplement traditional growth where water and fertilizers may not be readily available on a full-time basis"*. Following this conclusion, we installed 16 soil-based beds – 8 barrels per *Aqua-Pod*.

*There is no question that aquaponics will inevitably be a major part of protein and vegetation production in the near future. The question that remains is: Exactly how aquaponics can best be used? At CRA we contend that a mix of aquaponics and hydroponics – in a hybrid soil-based medium – may well offer the best use of resources available while providing the greatest variety and nutritional returns.*

Soil-based growth is much the same as hydroponic operations as only sterilized soil is used and then treated with nitrates from the aquaponic system(s), minerals and micro/macro constituents, Spanish moss for pest control and farm/home-generated compost.

Immediately upon starting and operating Rosa, it became apparent that if we intended to grow, while operating the farm with the least amount of labor hours, certain tasks had to be simplified to save time – hauling a hose around to top the sumps, feed/water soil-based plants and refill the systems following "change-outs" needed to be addressed. We began the installation of a mechanical plant with municipal water supplies, a central transfer pump, surface run piping and all related valves. In June 2010 the mechanical plant, serving Pee Wee and Rosa, was placed into service. The mechanical plant greatly reduces the operator's time and also saves water.

Construction of Big Boy commenced in early 2011. Big Boy is essentially the same design as Rosa and it is an all-screwed construction. Compiled data had proven the water chillers were not needed, so no chiller was installed on Big Boy (and the two existing chillers were removed from service). Big Boy was placed into service in March of 2011.

Hybrid soil-based beds were increased by 8, making a total of 24 beds, and the mechanical plant was expanded to meet the new demand. Two 275-gallon tanks were installed for treating municipal water supplies and storing the bio-filter as needed. We decided to install storage tanks to treat municipal supplies to eliminate chlorine and chloramines because, though chlorines can be gassed out of water over time or with mechanical agitation, chloramines must be removed chemically. At the time only one of the five local stations was utilizing chloramines – not the station supplying CRA R&D – but there was no guarantee that things would remain the same. Up to this time sodium thiosulfate had been used by compounding each individual tank/pond following a system change-out. The installation of the storage tanks and consolidating the water treatment process reduces time and costs.

With Big Boy up and running – fish growing and multiplying with good plant returns – we decided to return to Pee Wee and get it right. Pee Wee was rebuilt from the tank/pond tops up to reflect the construction of the larger *Aqua-Pod* units, while still using the same heavy PVC grow tubes with the original fluid return methods to the tank/ponds. Pee Wee remains what it was designed to be in our original mission statement. The Pee Wee design also remains available to any individual or organization that wishes to use the *Aqua-Pod* in providing the greatest nutritional return in the least amount of space to be placed in areas of the globe where travel from the home is difficult or dangerous and water scarce.

At this time there was more than enough farm production for food but: *Was there enough for research?* We decided to raise two more *Aqua-Pod*s in the least expensive manner possible. Construction of *Aqua-Pod* units #4 and #5 started in late March 2012.

*Aqua-Pod* units #4 and #5 are fastened – for the greater part – using a nail driver. The electrical supplies are slimmed down. Finding that insulation placed around the tanks/ponds was not needed (it deteriorated over time as it became wet) we didn't use any in units #4 and #5, though the aprons/skirts around the tanks/ponds were retained to ward off the effects of wind shear and for cosmetic reasons. The systems were placed in service four weeks later in early May 2012 along with 16 more hybrid soil-based beds and the added mechanical plant components.

***Aqua-Pods #4 and #5 Frames Constructed***

After running up units #4 and #5, research indicated that an excess of nitrates were being developed and distributed to the 40 aquaponically fed soil beds. With those findings in mind it was decided to add an additional 24 soil beds – 4 beds per *Aqua-Pod*. The soil beds were installed on additional ground covering, and related mechanicals were added for feeding/watering. The additional beds were completed in late May of 2012; totaling 64 hybrid soil-based beds.

Little else in terms of hardware has been done to the farm since late May 2012. The nailed parts of systems #4 and #5 were strengthened with screws at the points supporting the grow tubes on the distribution side – the horizontal supports were pulling away from the vertical components.

Following are the changes we made throughout the process:

- In the high heat of the summer fish were observed at the water surface and appeared to be gasping for air. Small air pumps (recommended for 40-gallon aquariums) were installed to assist in oxygenating the water.
- Initially 750-gallon-per-hour sump pumps were used, running on a full run-time basis. These have been replaced with float-activated 205-gallon-per-hour pumps running approximately 12 hours per day providing a 0.73 liter-per-hour flow rate per grow tube.
- Composting capacity has increased from one third of a cubic yard to one cubic yard.
- Seeding is primarily done in the *Aqua-Pod* units; little seeding is done in the seed beds. For use in the soil beds, the seeds are placed in a moist Jiffy Pod and placed in a net pot with clay pellets and germinated in a grow tube. Once the plant is established, the Jiffy Pod is removed and planted in the soil. This method provides for a 70 to 80-percent success rate in seed propagation.
- The only fish species in the *Aqua-Pod*s is tilapia. Other species have been removed and placed in aquariums or given away.
- It was decided that we would not attempt raising fresh water prawns. Our research, focusing on the plants, deemed that caring for two fish species was too time consuming.
- Electrical space heaters are no longer used in cold weather. Submerged heaters maintain water temperatures sufficient to maintain – for the most part – vegetative survival.
- The units – for the most part – are no longer fully covered in cold conditions. Only the northwest and northeast sides are covered on the outside *Aqua-Pod*s facing these two directions. If the units require a full covering, a two-foot-wide clear wrap can be wound about the units to seal in heat. Once installed,

the wrap remains in place for the entire cold season for cost savings. CRA has not had to use this option.

## Farm Operations

The tasks and time involved in the operation of the CRA farm are listed below. Specific instructions concerning each scheduled item can be reviewed in section "Operating the *Aqua-Pod* Garden". It's important the reader understand the time involved in the "farm" aspect of multiple *Aqua-Pods*. I have detailed the times involved in the expanded operation of 5 units and the related soil-based beds:

- Daily chores – 1/2 hour
- Every 3 to 4 Days – 1 ½ to 3 hours
- Weekly chores – 1 to 3 hours
- Weekly chores – optional – 2 to 3 hours

Concerning "change-outs" – if the rains have been good through the week and no change-outs have been done on a 3 to 4 day basis do a ⅓ rd system "change-out" to feed the soil-based beds and to reduce TDS of the *Aqua-Pod* units.

- Monthly – 5 hours
- Semi-annually (with no times estimated) – This discussion focuses on seeding and planting. Of the greatest importance is the maintenance of a healthy bio-filter and adequate vegetative growth to maintain the cycle. Interior growth – greenhouse or artificial lighting techniques – do not pose any challenges to harvesting, seeding and planting as these can be done throughout the year. Greenhouse installations will find – for the most part – more robust growth during the seasons with longer days but the fall and winter sunlight periods will not jeopardize a functioning bio-filter cycle. Exterior operations

are another matter depending on local conditions experienced. Heightened temperature and humidity – such as experienced at the CRA site – can make growing a number of plants difficult during the summer months. Operations in climates with monsoon seasons need to plant appropriately to weather harsh wet conditions thus maintaining a properly cycling bio-filter;

- Annual "clean and count" – 10 hours.

## Farm Growth Analysis

Keep in mind that these are duties outlined to operate five *Aqua-Pod* units and 64 hybrid soil-based beds. The times mentioned are to be considered the absolute minimum required to operate and maintain a farm of this size.

Crunching the above numbers we can see the *minimum* time required is a total of 773 hours/year; 64.5 hours/month; 15 hours/week; and, 2.1 hours/day *operating 5 Aqua-Pods and the related hybrid soil-based beds.* In each individual case there may not be a need to construct and operate that many units. Operating fewer units require less commitment of time.

As can be seen in the preceding: the operation of a small *Aqua-Pod* based farm doesn't take much time out of the operators schedule. To have an abundance of vegetables and proteins I would suggest one *Aqua-Pod* and related soil-based beds per three people operating year-round in a warm climate or interior operation. The family will not eat fish every day - once or twice a week - and everything will not be available all the time. But, with proper planning and a good seeding and planting schedule there will be enough to make the small amount of time required *freshly* rewarding!

## XI. Cleaning and Preparing Your Fish

*I have included this section in the manual because I have often been asked: "What is the best way to prepare my fish for consumption?" After "wrangling" with tilapia on several occasions I have found that "icing" them to sleep is the best method. A live tilapia can do serious harm with its very sharp fins and scales. Even in death they can jerk pretty hard when neural points are touched. Be careful the first several times working with your fish. Following a few tries you'll find it easy going and it doesn't take but a few minutes to gut and fillet a couple of fish.*

*Bon appétit!*

**11.1** Capture a fish or two and put them on ice. Tilapia are an active feisty fish and trying to clean one while it is alive can cause injury. There are some who bludgeon them into insensitivity but I think the process of icing them to sleep and then death is easier on both the fish and the preparer. It takes an hour on ice before the fish can be gutted, scaled and cleaned. In the mean time you'll need to line-up your knife of choice and a strong pair of scissors.

*Catch Your Fish...*

*... and Put it on Ice*

**11.2** Place the fish on a good cutting surface; preferably out of doors. Take the back edge of your knife and work up from the tail (against the scale pattern) and remove the scales on both sides of the fish.

***Remove the Fish Scales***

**11.3** Cut the pectoral fins, anal fin, anal spine, pelvic spines and pelvic fin away from the body; this will greatly assist in gutting and preparing the fish without injuring your hands.

*Remove the Fish Fins*

**11.4** Insert the point of a sharp knife into the belly just forward of the anus and slice up towards the head of the fish. Insert a finger and remove entrails by scooping them out and away from the incision. Wash the cavity with clean fresh water making sure it is fully evacuated.

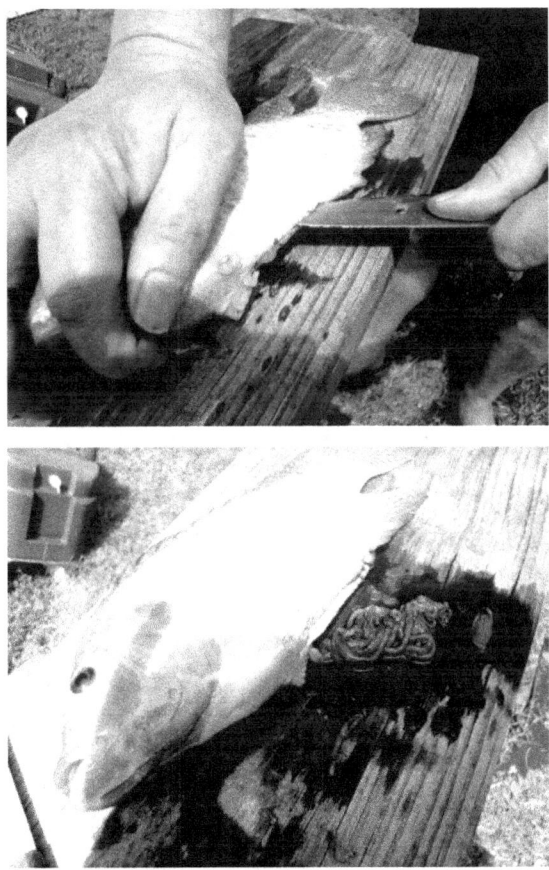

***Gut and Clean the Cavity***

**11.5** Cooking the fish whole requires no further cutting. The fish can be stuffed with herbs and roasted and the surface can be scored and seasoned. Cooking methods include smoking, baking, grilling and poaching.

**11.6** To fillet the fish cut into it diagonally just after the gills on both sides. Run the blade down into the fish until making firm contact with the bones. Penetrate the skin along the edge of the dorsal fin and gently slicing work the blade along the rib cage and separate the meat from the bone. Remove the fillet taking as much of the tail portion as possible. Use the same procedure to fillet the opposite side. Rinse the fillets and refrigerate/cool/freeze.

*Fillet Both Sides of Your Fish*

**11.7** The remaining carcass can be boiled to make a rich broth. It can be used like any other broth and, in our case, we feed some to our dogs over dry meal for increased protein and flavor. The rendered bones and head can be crushed and sown into the soil. Mix it down below the surface to prevent "critters" from digging up the garden.

**11.8** The fillets can be prepared a number of ways. Scoring and seasoning the skin side and cooking on the grill or frying make for a great meal. The skin can be removed and the fish prepared in sauces over pasta, couscous or rice as a curry, Mediterranean or Italian dish. It is also delicious in a soup or chowder. I'll be discussing more about the ways to prepare aquaponically raised fish and all the foods created in a later addition of *"Aquaponics in a Changing World"*.

*There has been a fair amount of discussion concerning how healthy tilapia is to eat in comparison to hamburger. The USDA "nutrition facts" calculates per 6 ounce serving of tilapia (a normal serving) values at 216 calories with 42 calories from fat. The USDA "nutrition facts" calculates per 6 ounce serving of hamburger (15% fat) at 420 calories with 220 calories from fat. Directly comparing these two examples one is hard pressed to think eating tilapia is "as bad" for a person as eating hamburger. Taking the protein values and "equaling" the two one concludes that 15.4 ounces of tilapia is required consumption to equal the value of a six ounce hamburger. 15.4 ounces of tilapia calculates to 544 calories with 107.8 calories from fat. That may provide an argument that tilapia is as unhealthy, or more unhealthy, to consume as hamburger. I present these facts for the reader to consider and draw their own conclusions. I will state that I don't think I've ever consumed more than 8 ounces of tilapia at any one time. I suppose tilapia, like hamburger, should be consumed in moderation but it seems hamburger would be best eaten in greater "moderation" than tilapia.*

*Of greater importance in consuming tilapia (or any other protein source) is the manner in which it is cultivated and raised. In our mission statement at CRA we stipulate "there be no high pressure feeding or production of fish"; meaning specifically that over-population and crowding in filthy conditions is not tolerated. What we are finding in large commercial "farm" operations are conditions that provide for over-population, disease and a foul tasting product. Consumption of fish raised in the proper manner is a much more important consideration than the nutritional values as compared to other food options.*

# XII. Glossary of Terms

- **≤:** Less than – or – equal to.
- **55 Gallon Holding Aquarium:** used when systems are evacuated and the tilapia are removed. The aquarium design permits close inspection of the fish observing color, any injuries or scarring and any mothers carrying eggs.
- **90° EL:** a 90° fitting in either socket or NPT styles.
- **AC:** Alternating Current, as opposed to DC (direct current), is the normal available grid supply.
- **Agriculture Extension Office:** A local entity – usually a government sponsored office – pooling agricultural information from educational institutes; business associations and financial institutes; and, farmer organizations and cooperatives. Information gathered and disseminated include crop options and times to plant; estimated demand and price projections; projected weather conditions; and, seed and plant acquisition options.
- **Ambient Temperature:** The natural existing temperature of the environment.
- **Ammonia:** The major component in the production of nitrogen fertilizers. Synthetic nitrogen, as used by Big Ag and many home gardeners, is produced by the "Haber-Bosch" process - an energy intensive process using natural gas and hydrogen to draw nitrogen from the atmosphere. In aquaponics ammonia, a by-product of fish breathing and body releases, is produced naturally.
- **Apron:** The apron, also referred as the "skirt", is paneling placed around the *Aqua-Pod* frame from the ground level up to the top of the Tank/ponds. It functions to mitigate the effects of wind shear and resulting rapid temperature swings. It also makes the *Aqua-Pod* more cosmetically appealing.

- **Aquaculture:** also known as "aqua-farming", is the farming of aquatic organisms such as fish, crustaceans, mollusks and aquatic plants.
- *Aqua-Pod*: An aquaponic growing unit utilizing minimum space with maximum output of proteins and vegetation.
- **AzaMax®:** A botanical insecticide, miticide and nematicide used to control harmful pests as a repellent, anti-feedant and insect growth regulator (IGR). It can be applied as a spray or the soil can be drenched. It is extremely harmful to aquaculture and must be used with caution by removing the plants from the *Aqua-Pod* and spraying away from the tank/ponds. AzaMax® is approved for use by the OMRI (Organic Materials Review Institute).
- **Back Blow:** A back blow is used to clear and clean return lines from the tank/ponds to the weir tank. A back blow is accomplished with a charged hose and nozzle applied to the tank/pond return port and pulsed to clear and clean the return line.
- **Bed Bundle:** The soil-based plants beds are bundled into 8 units each for ease of feeding/watering.
- **Big Ag:** Big Agricultural Commercial/Industrial Farming. Farming techniques utilizing extensive quantities of fossil fuels to operate equipment and to manufacture synthetic nitrogen fertilizers, pesticides and herbicides. Farm techniques using excessive quantities of water. Farming techniques returning excessive toxins to the water cycle, using pesticides the kill many beneficial insect and animal species and defoliants that destroy habitat for these same helpful species. Unsustainable farming techniques as water and fossil fuel stocks dwindle through over use.
- **Big Boy:** The 3rd aquaponic unit constructed and the 2nd *Aqua-Pod*.

- **Bio-filter:** The properly balanced cycle with developed nitrates and little to no traces of ammonia or nitrites.
- **Calorie (thermal calorie-cal):** A calorie is the amount of thermal energy required to raise the temperature of 1 cubic centimeter of distilled water (1 gram) 1 degree Celsius from 4°C to 5°C at sea level. The nutritional energy equivalent, often referred as calories, is actually a kilocalorie and is the energy required to heat 1 cubic liter of distilled water (1 kilogram) from 4°C to 5°C at sea level. One nutritional calorie equals 1000 thermal calories.
- **CFR's:** The U.S. "Code of Federal Regulations" is the final interpretation of bills passed in congress and signed into law by the president. CFR's address regulations in banking, maritime, industry, safety, education, food production and pollution - to name a very few – and provide the citizen and administrative and judicial branches of government guidance in interpreting the intent of the laws and the proper administration and enforcement of the law.
- **Chloramines:** A water disinfectant harmful to most aquaculture. Chloramines cannot be removed by "gassing off" and must be neutralized using a sodium thiosulfate based solution.
- **Chlorine:** A water disinfectant harmful to most aquaculture. Chlorine can be removed by "gassing off" or by using a sodium thiosulfate based solution.
- **Cichlids:** A family of fresh water fish naturally found in tropical America, Africa and Asia.
- **Clarity:** Visual "clarity" is a measure of how clear the water/effluent is. The fluids should be clear when placed in a glass or plastic container with a slight copper hue in color. Declining clarity indicates bio-filter problems and the cause must be addressed.

- **Compost:** n - A mixture of decaying organic matter, as from leaves and other vegetation wastes, used to improve soil structure and provide nutrients, v - To fertilize with a mixture of decaying organic matter.
- **CRA R&D:** Cyrson Ranch Aquaponics Research and Development.
- **Cross-growing:** A technique where seeds are propagated in the *Aqua-Pod* units and then transferred to soil-based bed and grown to maturity.
- **Cycling:** A term indicating an aquaponic system with a balanced "bio-filter". A "cycling" unit has little or no ammonia or nitrites present.
- **DC:** Direct Current as opposed to AC (alternating current). Most "alternative" power production – wind and solar voltaic – returns a DC supply that can be easily and economically stored in batteries for use when wind and solar are dormant. DC components – pumps and heaters – can be selected for operations or with the use of an DC/AC inverter; AC components can be used.
- **Distribution Manifold:** A manifold suspended above the Grow Tubes that receives its supply from the System Pump and supplies the Grow Tubes through lines by gravity effect.
- **Drench(ing):** The process of pouring a diluted substance – pest control or nutrients – over and into soil-based beds. It's a good practice between plantings to drench the soil beds with AzaMax® to assist in controlling pests;
- **Epsom salts:** A source of magnesium and an essential mineral in plant growth.
- **Gaza Strip:** A Palestinian Territory located on the Mediterranean Sea and bordered to the southwest by Egypt and to the east and north by Israel.

- **GMO:** A Genetically Modified Organism is an organism whose genetic material has been altered using genetic engineering techniques. GMO plants are modified for a number of reasons – to increase pest resistance; drought resistance; and, resistance to herbicides. The Monsanto® Corporation has developed a number of plant strains that when used with the herbicide Roundup® (glyphosate) are not affected while other plants – milkweed in particular – are destroyed by spraying the fields. Milkweed is the primary source of food for the Monarch butterfly larva on its annual journey from Mexico to North America. With the advent of GMO's and Roundup® the butterfly population has dwindled 59% in the past 10 years. The effects of GMO crops, and related herbicides and pesticides, on humans is not understood at this time. Due to questions about health effects of long term GMO interaction many nations, including the European Union, require rigorous testing and approval to grow GMO strains and require "truth in labeling" of all GMO products. The USA requires no testing or approval of GMO plant lines or any truth in labeling concerning GMO products.

- **Gravity Supply Manifold:** Also called the "Distribution Manifold" is the highest point in the fluid transfer system of an *Aqua-Pod*. Contents are received from the unit sump pump to the Gravity Supply Manifold and distributed, through flexible PVC tubing, to each of the 12 grow tubes.

- **Ground Cover:** Ground cover is a product utilized to minimize encroaching vegetation to the *Aqua-Pod* and soil-based beds systems.

- **Grow Tube:** One of 12 tubes in an *Aqua-Pod* unit used for placing pots with plants. Also called an "irrigation" tube.

- **Kilo-calorie (nutritional calorie-Cal):** A kilo-calorie is a nutritional energy equivalent, often referred as a "calorie", and is the energy required to raise the temperature of 1 cubic liter of distilled water (one kilogram) from 4° C to 5° C at sea level. One nutritional calorie equals 1000 "thermal" calories. A thermal calorie is the amount of energy required to raise the temperature of one cubic centimeter of distilled water (one gram) 1 degree from 4° C to 5° C at sea level.

- **Net Pot:** A plant pot with "net" design providing ability for nutrient up-take in grow tubes.
- **NFT:** Nutritional Flow Technique – A method of aquaponic design and operation.
- **Nitrates:** An essential nutrient for supplying plant growth. Nitrates are the ingredient produced in an aquaponic system with a properly cycling bio-filter.
- **Nitrosomonas:** A bacteria attracted to ammonia which converts ammonia into nitrites.
- **Nitrospira:** A bacteria attracted to nitrites which converts the nitrites to nitrates.
- **NPT:** National Pipe Thread. Threaded and tapered pipe and fittings.
- **Pee Wee:** A hybrid aquaponic unit and the 1st unit constructed at CRA R&D.
- **pH:** A measure of acidity and base. 14 point scales with 7 a neutral, 0 being the highest acidity and 14 the greatest alkalinity.
- **Pooling:** Pooling is a result of a grow tube obstruction – most often root growth – resulting in lost flow pattern and effluent running out of grow tube socket opening rather than returning to the tanks through the pipes as designed.
- **Prawn:** A fresh water species of prawn (or shrimp) researched as a possible aquaculture fish for development at CRA R&D. It was decided that tilapia was our fish of choice

and no further attempts have been made to acquire and grow prawn up to the time of this writing.

- **PVC:** Polyvinyl Chloride. The plastic-like substance used to make pipes and fittings.
- **Root Trimming:** Roots are trimmed monthly on mature plants in the *Aqua-Pod* grow tubes. Root trimming ensures steady flow through the grow tubes and speeds plant growth. Trimmed roots are fed to the fish or composted.
- **Rooting:** See "Root Trimming".
- **Rosa Parks:** The 2nd aquaponic unit constructed at CRA R&D. Rosa is the prototype for the *Aqua-Pod*.
- **Saddle:** The support(s) for the Gravity Distribution Manifold.
- **Skirt:** The skirt, also referred as the "apron", is paneling placed around the *Aqua-Pod* frame from the ground level up to the top of the tank/ponds. It functions to mitigate the effects of wind shear and resulting rapid temperature swings. It also makes the *Aqua-Pod* more cosmetically appealing.
- **Socket Fitting:** A fitting that accommodates glued or "sweated" fittings. Sweated fittings are not used in the construction of the *Aqua-Pod* or related gardens.
- **Socket:** A hole in grow tube that accommodates a 4" net pot for plant growth.
- **Sodium Thiosulfate:** A compound added to municipal water supplies to neutralize chlorine and chloramines. Chlorine and chloramines are harmful to most fresh water aquatic life.
- **Soil-Based Beds:** A hydroponic growing medium of sterilized soil treated with micronutrients and planted and fertilized with nitrates created in the *Aqua-Pod*.

- **Storage Tanks:** Tanks for storing treated water for use in systems. Also used to store bio-filter water to return to units following unit evacuation.
- **Sump Tank:** Tank capturing overflow from the Weir Tank. System pump and float controls are contained within Sump Tank.
- **Tampa Bay, Florida:** Located on the western & southern side of the state on the Gulf of Mexico and at latitude 27°95'N. Tampa is situated just above the Tropic of Cancer at 23°26'N.
- **Tank Net:** A custom constructed netting used to line the insides of each tank/pond in the *Aqua-Pod* systems. This has been removed and netting was discontinued in 2013.
- **Tank/Ponds:** Tanks holding aquaculture (fish) in the *Aqua-Pod* unit. This term is adopted throughout this manual to emphasize the aquaculture aspect of the *Aqua-Pod* operation. The tank/ponds phrase reminds the reader that live "pond" life is an integral part of the operation and to maintain a zero tolerance for senseless death of the aquaculture.
- **Tap (also "Thread" Tap):** A tool used to "tap" a component and form female thread pattern for the installation of a male threaded component (bolt or NPT pipe fitting).
- **TDS Meter:** An electrical meter that senses conductivity between two poles. As solids increase conductivity increases. Electrical output is scaled to read in parts per million (ppm) total dissolved solids.
- **TDS:** Total Dissolved Solids.
- **Teflon Tape:** A tape used on pipe fitting threads to make a leak proof seal.
- **Tilapia:** A cichlid species used primarily as a food fish. The only tilapia legal in Florida – the location of CRA R&D - is the Blue Tilapia.

- **Top Cover (also – Unit Cover Membrane):** The *Aqua-Pod* unit top covers are semi-clear membranes cut to size and installed 36" over the grow tubes. Top covers provide relief for seedlings during the harsh months of summer sun along with protection against acid rains, discouraging birds from feeding on the plants and reducing the introduction of harmful pests. During cold spells the top cover holds heat that is maintained with tank/pond heaters.
- **Transfer Pump:** A centrally located pump for transferring water and effluent throughout the farm.
- **Weir Tank:** Tank capturing overflow returns from *Aqua-Pod* tank/ponds.
- **Work Horse:** A term used to describe *Aqua-Pod* plants/vegetation providing the best nutrient up-take with the least amount of attention. Workhorses are "must" plants and vegetation for guaranteed maintenance of the bio-filter.

## XIII. Review Questions & Answers

### Aquaponics Defined

**1. NFT, as concerns aquaponics, stands for:**
    A.  Non Flexible Timing;
    B.  Nutrient Flow Technique;
    C.  National Field Training;
    D.  Nautical Funding Tribunal.

**2. How is "pooling" prevented in the *Aqua-Pod*?**
    A.  Plants are removed and the roots trimmed;
    B.  Pooling is never an issue;
    C.  Both A & B;
    D.  Neither A or B.

**3. Managing Nitrates environmentally can be accomplished by:**
    A.  Increasing or decreasing aquatic populations
    B.  Increasing or decreasing aquaponic plant production
    C.  Increasing or decreasing aquaponically fed soil-based plant production
    D.  All of the above

**4. The incorporation of soil-based – aquaponically fed - plant growth increases water consumption by:**
    A.  $\leq 2\%$
    B.  $\leq 4\%$
    C.  $\leq 8\%$
    D.  $\leq 12\%$

**5. Which of the following are common aquaponic applications for plant growth?**
    A.  Deep water raft
    B.  Recirculating systems
    C.  Reciprocating systems
    D.  All of the above

## 6. The bacteria that convert ammonia to nitrites are named:

A. Nitrosomonas

B. Nitrobacter

C. Nitrobylia

D. Nitro glycerin

## 7. In the *Aqua-Pod* the net pots are submerged into effluent flow:

A. 2" to 4"

B. 1" to 3 ½"

C. 1 ¼" to 1 ½"

D. ¼" to 3/8"

## 8. Which, of the following components, are added to the *Aqua-Pod*?

A. Calcium

B. Potassium

C. Iron

D. Magnesium

E. All of the above

## 9. pH in the *Aqua-Pod* is found to run:

A. 4.6 to 5.1

B. 5.1 to 5.7

C. 7.0 to 7.6

D. 7.1 to 7.9

## Cyrson Ranch Aquaponics R&D - The History

## 1. The major goal in creating and designing the *Aqua-Pod* was to:

A. Grow Pea's using fish and water

B. Grow plants and fish on the smallest physical footprint

C. Develop a "stand alone" growing platform

D. Both B &C

## 2. Aquaponics is:

A.  The husbandry of plants and fish
B.  A new video game
C.  A kind of underwater sound system
D.  Surgery techniques done in the water

**3. In comparison to industrial growing techniques CRA R&D uses:**

A.  88% of the water
B.  28% of the water
C.  18% of the water
D.  6% of the water

**4. How much of each energy dollar goes to the purchase of fertilizer and pesticides in industrial farming methods:**

A.  60₵
B.  48.2₵
C.  35.5₵
D.  20₵

**5. A Bio-Filter is:**

A.  A filter installed in your car
B.  A computer program that helps with tough biology questions
C.  The story of a filter
D.  A system that converts ammonia and nitrites to nitrates that plants take up as food

**6. Industrial agriculture uses:**

A.  8% of the planet's fresh water
B.  24% of the planet's fresh water
C.  45% of the planet's fresh water
D.  70% of the planet's fresh water

**7. Industrial Pesticides have been suspected in the following:**

A.  Plummeting populations of honey bees nationwide
B.  Gender manipulation turning male frogs into female frogs
C.  A dramatic increase bat deaths

    D.  All of the above

## 8. The Gaza Strip is located:
    A.  In an adult dance club in Tampa, Florida
    B.  On the eastern coast of the Mediterranean Sea
    C.  Next to Sunset Beach
    D.  At a race track in Detroit, Michigan

## 9. The aquaponic cycle includes:
    A.  Fish
    B.  Plants
    C.  Microbes
    D.  All of the above

## 10. "Zero Tolerance" in aquaponics means:
    A.  No tolerance concerning the needless death of the aquaculture
    B.  No usage of mind altering drugs on the fish
    C.  No drug usage by the farmers and care-takers
    D.  No dissenting opinions expressed on the farm

## Constructing the *Aqua-Pod*

## 1. The *Aqua-Pod* consists of:
    A.  3 tank/ponds
    B.  12 grow tubes
    C.  A diving board
    D.  A & B

## 2. The *Aqua-Pod* foot print size is closest to:
    A.  80 square feet
    B.  63 square feet
    C.  52 square feet
    D.  38 square feet

## 3. In the construction of the *Aqua-Pod* – how many return flow piping supports are required and at what length?

A. 4 at 80"

B. 2 at 59"

C. 6 at 10'

D. There are no return flow piping supports used in the *Aqua-Pod*

**4. On a standard piece of paper place a ruler and draw a line from the 1" mark to the 10" mark. The length of this line is:**

A. 7 inches

B. 8 inches

C. 9 inches

D. 10 inches

**5. On the same piece of paper place the ruler and draw a line from the 1 ½" mark to the 8 ½" mark. The length of this line is:**

A. 6 inches

B. 7 inches

C. 8 ½ inches

D. 9 ½ inches

**6. On the same piece of paper place the ruler and draw a line from the 1 ¼" mark to the 9 ½" mark. The length of this line is:**

A. 7 inches

B. 9 ½ inches

C. 8 ¼ inches

D. 9 inches

**7. NPT stands for:**

A. Not Playing Today

B. North Point Traditions

C. National Pipe Thread

D. Naval Positioning Tactics

**8. The *Aqua-Pod* is constructed in a "fail safe" manner meaning:**

A. It can't shoot nuclear missiles

B. Aquaculture cannot be killed by accidently pumping the water out

C. B only

D. Both A & B

### 9. An "off the shelf" component means:

A. A component available to anyone anywhere

B. Something that fell off the shelf

C. An item from the sea shelf floor

D. A component cut from the end of a shelf

### 10. When we discuss using a "clear" cut of lumber – What do we mean?

A. One can see through the wood

B. The lumber can be understood

C. There are no knots in the wood

D. Its checks won't bounce

### 11. Dimension Lumber is kiln dried. What are the actual dimensions of a 2" by 8" piece of lumber?

A. 2" x 8"

B. 1 ¾" x 7 ¾"

C. 1 ½" x 7 ¼"

D. 1 ¼" x 7 ½"

### 12. What electrical components are required for *Aqua-Pod* operations?

A. Air pumps – constant use

B. Sump Pump – intermittent use

C. Tank/ponds heaters – used in cold weather

D. All of the above

### 13. The *Aqua-Pod* electrical supply requires what of the following?

A. GFI (ground fault interrupted) outlets

B. Installation and use to National and local codes

C. All electrical cords to be proper with no fraying of the insulation

D. All of the above

## 14. When questions arise concerning use of electricity:

    A.   Call your mother

    B.   Ask the guy down the street who seems good at electricity

    C.   Consult with a licensed electrician

    D.   Don't give it another thought

## 15. Safety glasses should be used at all times in construction of the *Aqua-Pod*. Where are safety glasses kept while on site?

    A.   Folded up and hung in your shirt just under your chin where they look sexy

    B.   On your head – backwards – so they look real sexy

    C.   ON YOUR FACE AND OVER YOUR EYES

    D.   In your lunch box

## 16. If an electrical tool cord exhibits frayed insulation:

    A.   Get some electrical tape and tape the frayed parts

    B.   Make sure everyone knows not to touch the cord at the frayed part

    C.   Keep it a secret – the chances of anyone getting hurt are probably pretty slim

    D.   Remove the tool until it can be repaired or replaced

## 17. When a person is working on a ladder a "spotter" is required. If you are the "spotter" what are your responsibilities?

    A.   Make sure the person making lemonade gets it sweet enough

    B.   Talking to that girl/guy you really like

    C.   Paying full attention to the person on the ladder – their needs, observing balance, protecting the person from other activities that might injure them and insuring the ladder remains safely placed

    D.   Talking on the phone

## 18. If you are not quite sure what you are doing or are supposed to do:

    A.   Do it anyhow – it's no big deal if it's wrong

B.   Stop and get assistance and guidance

C.   Don't do anything and go make a telephone call to your best friend

D.   Do something entirely different – after all it's a free country

## The *Aqua-Pod-* Starting the System

**1. Chlorine and chloramines added to municipal water supplies must be removed prior to use in the *Aqua-Pod* because:**

A.   The fish don't have teeth and don't need chlorine or chloramines

B.   The chlorine and/or chloramines will bleach the plants white

C.   Chlorines and/or chloramines are toxic to fish and could kill them

D.   None of the above

**2. The *Aqua-Pod* has a mandatory "change-out" at what level of TDS?**

A.   210 PPM

B.   255 PPM

C.   280 PPM

D.   320 PPM

**3. At start-up of the *Aqua-Pod* what tools are available to analyze the development of the Bio-Filter?**

A.   pH levels

B.   TDS (Total Dissolved Solids)

C.   A sense of smell

D.   All of the above

**4. Initial start-up of the *Aqua-Pod* requires what type of plants?**

A.   Plant with good "take-up" qualities

B.   Hearty plants

    C.  Flowers

    D.  A & B

## 5. What cautions must be taken when purchasing items designed for hydroponic farmers?

    A.  Watch for DEA officials as hydroponics is used to grow illegal plants

    B.  Many hydroponic products have harmful chemicals and fertilizers embedded

    C.  There is no need to worry using hydroponic products in aquaponic systems

    D.  None of the above

## 6. The bacteria that convert ammonia to nitrites are named:

    A.  Nitrosomonas

    B.  Nitrobacter

    C.  Nitrobylia

    D.  Nitro glycerin

## 7. What can be used to increase acidity (lower alkalinity) in the *Aqua-Pod*?

    A.  Car battery acid

    B.  Pure distilled white vinegar

    C.  Moldy donuts

    D.  Tomato juice

## 8. What can be used to increase alkalinity (lower acidity) in the *Aqua-Pod*?

    A.  Baking soda

    B.  Baking powder

    C.  Coffee

    D.  Moldy donuts

## 9. When adjusting pH levels in the *Aqua-Pod* system what rate of change is best?

    A.  10 points per week

    B.  5 points per day

   C. .1 point per day

   D. None of the above

## Soil-Based Installation

**1. The goals in developing the *Aqua-Pod* platform include:**

   A. The greatest nutritional return on the smallest possible footprint

   B. Durability and longevity

   C. Flexibility and variety in plants and vegetation produced

   D. A high level of control for the operator

   E. All of the above

**2. Plants can be grown using nitrates generated in an *Aqua-Pod* by:**

   A. Growing in "plant wool"

   B. Growing in vertical beds

   C. Growing in sterilized and treated soils

   D. All of the above

**3. Placing ground cover helps to:**

   A. Provide ease of grounds maintenance

   B. Prevent local pests from invading aquaponically fed soil beds

   C. Neither A or B

   D. Both A & B

**4. Soil-based plants require minerals. Which of the following are added to the soil?**

   A. Hydrated lime

   B. Muriate of potash

   C. Chelated iron

   D. Epsom salts

   E. All of the above

**5. AzaMax:**
    A.  Is used to max the Aza
    B.  To minimize pests
    C.  Cannot be in contact with the tank/ponds
    D.  B & C

**6. When is it required to use a Sodium Thiosulfate solution to treat water with chlorine and chloramines?**
    A.  Following a tank/ponds "change-out"
    B.  When topping the sump in the morning
    C.  When topping the sump in the evening
    D.  None of the above

**7. Garden pests can be discouraged by:**
    A.  Leaving lady bugs, spiders, praying mantissas and frogs alone
    B.  Placing reflective disks under plants to reflect light up under the leaves
    C.  Mechanically removing and destroying harmful pests
    D.  Growing plants pests don't like and stay away from
    E.  All of the above

**8. When a butterfly cocoon or lava is discovered**
    A.  Yell EEK! And kill them by squishing them
    B.  Consolidate cocoons and larva in one soil bed
    C.  Remove the plant(s) to an isolated soil bed and let them mature and fly away
    D.  B & C

**9. What does CFR stand for?**
    A.  Captain From Raleigh
    B.  Capturing Free Range
    C.  Code of Federal Regulations
    D.  Colin Fritz Romeo

**10. Composting materials can be:**
    A.  Household vegetable wastes

B. Farm debris

C. Warm blooded animal wastes

D. Citrus wastes

E. A & B only

## Operating the *Aqua-Pod* Garden

**1. Daily testing of the system includes:**
  A. Taking pH readings
  B. Testing TDS
  C. Checking water clarity
  D. All of the above

**2. Feed the fish in the *Aqua-Pod*:**
  A. A quality fish food of the correct size for the size fish in the system
  B. Duckweed in the evening
  C. Solid pellets and ground pellets once per day in the morning
  D. All of the above

**3. Daily items in maintenance of the *Aqua-Pod* and garden include:**
  A. Feeding the fish
  B. "Topping" the *Aqua-Pod*
  C. Harvesting vegetables and fish for consumption
  D. All of the above

**4. Weekly items to be done include adding the following to the pump sump:**
  A. Potassium – Muriate of Potash
  B. Calcium – Horticulture Hydrated Lime
  C. Magnesium – Epsom Salts
  D. Iron – Chelated Iron
  E. All of the above

**5. Good sources of seed and plants are available:**
   A.  By buying local produce and saving seed to plant
   B.  By bringing plants grown to seed and saving to re-seed
   C.  From local seed/plant swap clubs
   D.  All of the above

**6. What is needed for the annual "clean and count" process?**
   A.  A holding tank to place fish for observation and counting
   B.  A barrel to save off 50(+) gallons of Bio-Filter effluent
   C.  A submergible pump to evacuate tank/ponds
   D.  All of the above

**7. Why don't we clean the *Aqua-Pod* tank/ponds with soaps and detergents?**
   A.  It can compromise the Bio-Filter upon returning the units to service
   B.  It can destroy the Bio-Filter upon returning the units to service
   C.  It's no problem – clean away
   D.  A and B

**8. During the "annual clean and count" it is recommended the fish be moved off to a 55 gallon aquarium for what purpose?**
   A.  To observe any female carrying eggs in her mouth
   B.  To easily size and count the fish
   C.  To observe for any injuries or disease
   D.  All of the above

**9. Why is it important to transfer fish between tanks of like temperatures?**
   A.  Extreme temperature changes can weaken the fish making them susceptible to illness
   B.  Extreme temperature changes can shock the fish resulting in death
   C.  Neither A or B
   D.  Both A and B

**10. Why do tilapias eat their young?**
- A. They are a yummy snack
- B. Many tilapia, like many people, don't like kids
- C. Tilapia are of the opinion that fry should be eaten and not heard
- D. Tilapia eats its offspring to maintain a population to match the environment

## Plant Selection, Acquisition & Seeding

**1. Growing industrial crops in Florida requires:**
- A. Large amounts of water
- B. Large quantities of fertilizers
- C. Large quantities of pesticides and herbicides
- D. All of the above

**2. When a plant suggested for growth in the *Aqua-Pod* is described as a "work horse" what is meant?**
- A. The plant can pull lots of weight
- B. The plant can take up a lot of ammonia, nitrites and nitrates
- C. The plant looks like a horse
- D. None of the above

**3. Which of the following are ways to acquire seeds and plants for growing in the *Aqua-Pod* and on the farm?**
- A. Purchase seeds and plants from box stores and nurseries
- B. Purchase seed from seed catalogs
- C. Save seed from locally bought produce
- D. Save seed from plants grown on the farm
- E. All of the above

**4. Help is available in determining plants to grow in the *Aqua-Pod* and on the farm by:**
- A. Consulting with the local agriculture extension office
- B. Visiting local farmers' markets

    C.   Participating in local plant and seed swaps

    D.   All of the above

**5. What are some problems with the use of GMO seeds?**

    A.   The effects of GMO plants and products on humans is still unknown

    B.   GMO seeds are required to be purchased yearly and re-use of "captured" seed is illegal

    C.   GMO crops can cross pollinate non GMO crops

    D.   All of the above

**6. What is recommended for storing seed?**

    A.   Store in air tight containers or bags

    B.   Store in a refrigerator away from the freezer section

    C.   Bring up to room temperature before opening the air tight container

    D.   Do not use if stored over 3 years

    E.   All of the above

**7. Melons, squashes and cucumbers can be difficult to grow because of:**

    A.   Aphids

    B.   Leaf miners

    C.   Both A & B

    D.   Neither A or B

**8. Which of the following is true?**

    A.   Tomatoes can be grow up to a year on the same plant

    B.   Lettuce can last long after industrial methods by picking leafs daily

    C.   Herbs and spices need only to be pruned and cut back and do not need replanting

    D.   All of the above

## CRA Farm Layout - Growing Your Operation

**1. Concerning the *Aqua-Pod* – Which of the following statements are true?**
  A. Each *Aqua-Pod* has 3 – 150 gallon tank/ponds
  B. There are 12 grow tubes in each *Aqua-Pod*
  C. There are 216 sockets for 4" net pots in each *Aqua-Pod*
  D. All the above

**2. What are some of the time saving features installed at the CRA R&D center?**
  A. Centralized feed/water transfer pump
  B. Transfer piping to feed/water soil-based beds
  C. Large storage tanks piped into transfer system to store and treat water
  D. Municipal water piped directly to top the individual *Aqua-Pod* sumps
  E. Overhead run electrical supply cables
  F. All of the above

**3. Pee Wee – the first NFT platform constructed at CRA R&D is different from the *Aqua-Pod*. How so?**
  A. Pee Wee has only 2 tank/ponds
  B. Pee Wee uses a different method to return effluent to the tank/ponds
  C. Pee Wee's grow tubes are a different schedule and, in 50%, different sizes
  D. All of the above

**4. Pee Wee was designed to:**
  A. Provide a platform to produce protein and vegetables with the greatest nutritional value while utilizing the least amount of space
  B. Provide a food source at, or close to, the home to mitigate travel in restricted hazardous and dangerous environments

C. Provide a nutrition source for use where water is scarce and power intermittent

D. All of the above

**5. Pee Wee is:**

A. Pre-assembled and then dismantled and shipped for field assembly

B. Packed in a manner so 4 people can lift and move the package

C. Packed to permit transportation on an animal drawn cart or a flatbed truck

D. All of the above

**6. The *Aqua-Pod* was born:**

A. When a seed of the "aqua" was planted

B. After mating Pee Wee with Big Boy

C. Upon the successful construction and operation of Rosa Parks

D. None of the above

**7. Why was it decided to increase production using soil-based – aquaponically fed – grow beds?**

A. It met with the original CRA R&D mission statement

B. It provided a flexible manner in which the bio-filter could be managed

C. It increased research by providing alternate grow platforms to compare returns

D. All of the above

**8. Soil-based – aquaponically fed – beds have what of the following characteristics?**

A. They use sterilized soil to reduce migration of pests

B. They are treated with minerals

C. They use Spanish moss for pest control

D. They use sterilized cow manure and compost for additional nutrition

E. All of the above

## 9. What are some of the reasons aquaponics will become a major supply of vegetables and proteins?

A. Aquaponics uses just 2% to 6% of the water currently used in industrial Big Ag operations

B. Water is becoming scarcer and scarcer as the results of global climate change increase

C. Aquaponics uses no synthetic fertilizers that require vast quantities of natural gas to produce

D. As stores of natural gas recede the ability to make synthetic fertilizers will be reduced

E. The US EPA reports that 75% of the pollutants introduced into out streams, rivers and lakes come from industrial Big Ag operations

F. With the limited water usage in aquaponic farming runoff is virtually eliminated

G. The amount of environmental damage by industrial pesticides and herbicides will result in the eventual banning of these substances

H. Aquaponics do not use, and cannot use, these products

I. All of the above

## 10. Creating a "mechanical plant" provides what advantage(s)?

A. Reduced time in topping sumps

B. Reduced time and effort when feeding/watering soil-based beds

C. Reduced time and effort when doing system change-outs

D. All of the above

## 11. Two 275 gallon storage tanks located at the CRA R&D site are for:

A. Treating water with sodium thiosulfate to eliminate chlorine and chloramines

B. Holding Bio-Filter when evacuating an *Aqua-Pod* unit

C. Use in an emergency if water supply is lost

D. A & B

**12. Units #4 and #5 were constructed with lower costs. What are some of the cost saving methods?**

A. They are constructed – for the most part – using a power nailer

B. Electrical service is slimmed down

C. Tank/ponds insulation was left out

D. All of the above

**13. Using a ground cover offers what advantages?**

A. Decreases time required to maintain plant growth around the units and soil beds

B. Eliminates intrusion of native roots in the soil beds

C. Reduces introduction of local plant seed into soil beds and grow tubes

D. All of the above

**14. What are some advantages of composting?**

A. Compost provides an additional source of plant nutrients

B. Composting uses farm/home wastes and reduces that carried away to landfills

C. It saves on costs related to purchasing soil

D. All of the above

**15. Some items accomplished weekly include:**

A. Renew the filter at the weir overflow

B. Compound the systems with minerals

C. Feed the composters

D. Weed the soil beds

E. Start seed as required

F. Prep seed for drying

G. Bag, tag and store dried seed

H. All of the above

**16. "Family Farming" in aquaponics becomes viable due to which of the following?**

  A.  Greater returns are derived from growing and selling both fish and vegetables
  B.  Input costs in aquaponics are significantly less than industrial Big Ag operations
  C.  Aquaponically grown foods are gaining appeal because they are truly organic, sustainable and locally produced
  D.  All of the above

## XII. Answers to Section Follow-up Questions

### III. Aquaponics Defined

   1) B; 2) A; 3) D; 4) A; 5) D; 6) A; 7) C; 8) D; 9 C

### IV. Cyrson Ranch Aquaponics R&D - The History

   1) D; 2) A; 3) D; 4) D; 5) D; 6) D; 7) D; 8) B; 9) D; 10)

### V. Constructing the *Aqua-Pod*

   1) D; 2) C; 3) B; 4) C; 5) B; 6) C; 7) C; 8) B; 9) A; 10) C; 11) C; 12) D; 13) D; 14) C; 15) C; 16) D; 17) C; 18) B

### VI. The *Aqua-Pod* – Starting the System

   1) C; 2) D; 3) D; 4) D; 5) B; 6) A; 7) B; 8) A; 9) C

### VII. Soil-Based Bed Installation

   1) E; 2) D; 3) D; 4) E; 5) D; 6) A; 7) E; 8) D; 9) C; 10) E

## VIII. Operating the *Aqua-Pod* Garden

1) D; 2) D; 3) D; 4) D; 5) D; 6) D; 7) D; 8) D; 9) D; 10) D

## IX. Plant Selection, Acquisition and Seeding

1) D; 2) C; 3) E; 4) D; 5) D; 6) E; 7) D; 8) D

## X. CRA Farm Layout Details – Grow Your Operation

1) A; 2) F; 3) D; 4) D; 5) D; 6) C; 7) D; 8) E; 9) E; 10) D; 11) D; 12) D; 13) D; 14) D; 15) H; 16 D

## XIV. FAQ's and Trouble Shooting Tips

### The *Aqua-Pod* Construction Details:

### You emphasize placing a ground cover under the *Aqua-Pod* and soil-based hydroponic planters. Why?

Ground covering helps in several ways. It reduces efforts in managing native growth and it reduces the introduction of native seed in the soil-based beds and *Aqua-Pod* grow tubes. CRA R&D is located just above the Tropic of Cancer and native growth is quite aggressive.

### How do I "pick" my wood for construction?

Back before the advent of the "box store" there were a number of privately owned yards where one could go and either have a wood order filled or, at least, work with competent employees who would assist in the selection of the wood to meet the project at hand. Those days have long passed and though the prices paid at a "box store" seem less the reality is the purchaser in on her/his own when selecting wood. All of the pieces selected are of 2 x 4", 2 x 6" and 2 x 8" dimensions and will be of a #2 grade. Inspect each piece by "eying" the length. Reject any piece exhibiting a "bowing" or "sagging" action. Observe any knots and try and stay away from any that might be "popping" and any piece with excessive knots along the edge of the wood (knots are difficult to nail/screw through). If the wood is gouged or otherwise damaged in manufacturing or shipping put it to the side. The 2 x 8" board needs 2 – 16" lengths "clear" of knots. After checking the 2 x 8" piece as instructed above scope out the 2 - 16" pieces you will cut and modify for the Supply Manifold Support. Save the receipts to return any wood (that hasn't been cut) for replacement or refund.

The wood doesn't have to perfect. There's only so much wood to be had in the world even as "sustainable" amounts are "re-grown". An experienced carpenter can use wood cuts that a novice will find difficult to work with and will leave the best behind if not required. The *Aqua-Pod* - correctly constructed - will last 20(+) years. Pick materials you are confident working with.

**You talk about "ripping" wood. Please explain.**

In construction of the *Aqua-Pod* there are 3 types of wood cuts involved. A "ripped" cut involves cutting with the grain of the wood – usually a length-wise cut. A "ripped" cut is best accomplished using a table saw with an adjustable "rip fence". Constructing the 16" Supply Manifold Support requires a rip cut using a jig saw. Another cut required in the construction of the *Aqua-Pod* is the "cross" cut. The "cross" cut goes against the grain and can be accomplished using a miter saw (chop saw), compound miter saw, hand radial saw or a jig saw. The final cut used in the construction of the *Aqua-Pod* is a "scroll" cut using a jig saw with a scrolling blade.

**Why do you suggest galvanized screws?**

Galvanized screws resist the effects of moisture & the elements; preventing rust and failure.

**You mention throughout the construction procedures placing the 3 tanks into the unit. Why?**

The structure must be assembled to fit the tanks. The tanks cannot be made smaller. Check to ensure the tanks fit and make corrections to the frame-work if necessary.

**I'm having trouble "plumbing" the frame horizontally and/or vertically. How do I correct for true?**

Vertical plumb is best achieved by pushing the upper vertical surfaces to true. Observe the position of the base when truing and, if required, hit the base with several whacks of a heavy hammer. Check the security of any clamps installed throughout this process and if needed, adjust the clamps. Once the verticals are trued recheck the horizontals and loosen/re-clamp – one at a time – until all are true. Recheck the verticals.

"Raising" the *Aqua-Pod* frame it can be a rather tedious affair working alone. I recommend at least two people and it's even better with four.

**Screwing as opposed to nailing the frame is mentioned several times. What are the advantages of each?**
Both methods have advantages and drawbacks. Screwing offers increased strength. If the unit is constructed in one location and then taken elsewhere – trailer or flatbed – screwing is required. Screwing also permits easy disassembly if the system is to be crated and shipped or if any modifications are required. On the downside, screws cost more than nails and time is consumed pre-drilling the wood prior to screwing. Nailing is fast and inexpensive. Nails are difficult to remove if a mistake is made ("ripping it out" – any carpenter will attest to that) and the unit does not hold up as well as a screwed *Aqua-Pod* if shifting or vibration is involved. If the unit is to be constructed on the spot where it is to be operated nailing works well with several exceptions as detailed.

**Can I use other tank/ponds than what you recommend in the construction of the *Aqua-Pod*?**
No.

**What is National Pipe Thread (NPT)?**

These are pipe fittings – male and female – used to assemble components of the hydraulics of the *Aqua-Pod*. Specific construction components used are ½", ¾" and 1 ¼" sizes. The NPT has a taper (as opposed to a "straight" thread nut/bolt) of ¾" per foot ensuring a water tight fit when properly assembled.

**You claim the *Aqua-Pod* is "fail-safe". What does that mean?**

The returns to the sump from the tanks are through the height in the tanks which overflow into the weir and from the weir to the sump tank where the pump takes suction. If the pump were to fail – either by stopping or if the pump does not shut-off properly – the tanks cannot lose level resulting in the potential harm or death to the fish. The tanks simply remain at the top – the overflow level – where the aquaculture remains unharmed. This condition can be maintained for days if necessary. Nothing is truly "fail-safe" and if the return piping from the tanks to the weir tank – piping and fittings below the tank-tops – were to fail the water could drain away and the fish harmed or killed. This is why it's important upon assembly to get it right and leak check prior to placing the unit in service.

**I left my PVC glue out overnight and it has a "gloppy" texture – not smooth. Can I use it?**

No.

**After cleaning and gluing PVC how long should I wait to put water to the piping?**

24 hours.

**The overflow line to the weir tank – you suggest not gluing it. Why?**

This permits the line to be removed and "back blown" with a pressurized hose.

**The sockets holding the net pots are offset 2" between each pipe. Why?**

This permits less "crowding" of plants in the unit.

**Grow tube caps are glued onto the pipes. They are then caulked. Why?**

To ensure water tight integrity.

**Why is Teflon tape applied to pipe threads?**

To ensure water tight integrity.

**The weir bucket leaks at the overflow at the hole in the weir. Why?**

This could be caused by several factors. If you "wallowed" the ¾" hole through the tank a seal will be difficult to achieve. If that is the case try to place a larger "O" ring in service. One can be obtained at an auto parts store. Also, the male threaded coupling might not be screwed tightly into the female threaded coupling. Try re-tightening.

**The manifold supply lines are installed but I have some leakage at the barb fittings. What do I do?**

The flexible PVC is not sized correctly. You will probably be required to install ⅜" to ⅞" hose clamps and tighten to stop leakage. The major manufacturing for flexible PVC is for "sprinkler" system and drip water irrigation. The products change constantly (both barb fittings and hose) and adaptation may be required.

**Are Unit Top Covers required?**

Not necessarily. If the unit is to be positioned inside a structure – greenhouse or artificial lighting – there is no need for the top covers, If the unit is to be built for outdoor use it is highly recommended the top covers are installed. Top covers decrease the effects of acid rain, the intrusion by birds, falling and blowing seed and harmful insects. Top covers also temper the effects of intense periods of sunlight.

**You stipulate the specific use of Tuflex - UltraVinyl. Can another product be used?**

Yes. The Tuflex – UltraVinyl was selected following extensive research of a variety of possibilities and was chosen for its durability. CRA R&D is located in the Tampa Bay Florida region of the USA. The systems are subject to high winds and strong UV rays. Less expensive top cover options are available but CRA R&D operates on a "no fail" premise and the top covers selected have performed 100% over the past seven(+) years.

**Do the *Aqua-Pod* units require the use of tank/ponds apron/skirts?**

No. The apron/skirts provide tank/pond insulation against wind shear and make the unit more aesthetically pleasing in appearance. The apron/skirts are not required in more southern climates (and those located closer to the equator) as low temperature wind shear becomes a moot topic and when aesthetics have no bearing. Apron/skirts are not required for interior – greenhouse and artificial lighting – operations.

**What are some options as far as acquiring help the construct the *Aqua-Pod*?**

There are numerous possibilities for gathering assistance in construction. Aquaponics has, and continues, to interest and infect the world community. It's best to create a small mission plan, layout a flexible schedule and approach members of the community. There is a wealth of talent – senior citizen's groups have carpentry and shop clubs as do many churches, temples and mosques. High schools, community colleges and universities have shops, tools and talent and students can obtain knowledge and even credits helping. Growing food is fascinating and growing food in a sustainable manner is that much more satisfying. Plan, schedule and ask of those in the community - they will come!

**CRA R&D used all "new" components in its construction. Are new components a requirement?**

No. CRA R&D uses all new components due to research requirements – any failures required correction and the use of "new" materials negated forensic analysis of "used" component failures. There are a number of outlets where "used" materials – tanks, piping, pumps, heaters, observation aquariums – can be obtained for as little as 15₡ on the dollar. On-line sources include Craig's List to name but one. Placing a note on a board at aquarium stores is another way to acquire materials. There are "recycling yards" springing up throughout the world where new and used PVC piping, PVC components, barrels and storage tanks are sold. The secret to creating the system with "used" components it to buy two (or three) of any component above that needed on a day to day basis. That way – if a component fails - there is a "spare" for immediate installation.

**It is suggested that "color coded" PVC cleaners and glues be utilized. Why?**

Properly used color coded cleaners and glues eliminate the guess work concerning whether the joint has been properly treated and assembled. It's particularly important when more than one person is doing the assembly or if the assembly is done over time. Remember – if a joint is incorrectly assembled the chance of draining the system increases dramatically along with the possible death of the aquaculture.

**There is a list of "consolidated" tools. I don't understand several mentioned. What is a "Utility Knife"?**

Go to the library or the internet to find out about tools – or anything else in this text – that is not sufficient in detail. Or contact the author if required - aqua.podcra@gmail.com.

## The *Aqua-Pod* – Starting the System:

### Please explain "Bio-Filter". Where does the "Bio-Filter" exist in an aquaponic system?

There has been a lot written about the bio-filter and for the most part it's confusing and often appears more complex than it really needs to be. Once established the bio-filter exists throughout the entirety of the aquaponic system. For lack of a better term the bio-filter is the odorless "slime" felt on tank surfaces, grow tube surfaces and on the fish. The bio-filter is what makes fish difficult to handle because it makes them slippery. A successful bio-filter takes ammonia created by fish gills and excrement and converts it to nitrites which are converted to nitrates which plants need and readily take up as nutrients. The two primary bacteria involved are nitrosomonas and nitrospira and it is required that they be present and preserved. To strengthen the bio-filter – to fortify it against environmental swings – a reservoir is often created using solids such as rocks, pebbles, synthetic wools and even tight meshed screens - this is often, erroneously, termed the bio-filter. In the *Aqua-Pod* the bio-filter "reservoir" is contained in the several thousands of pellets used in the net-pots situated in the grow tube sockets.

### Explain the Bio-Filter, and how it works, in the *Aqua-Pod*.

The *Aqua-Pod* is a recirculating aquaponic system and, as mentioned previously, the bio-filter exists throughout the unit on a continuous basis. The reservoir providing bio-filter strength and flexibility lies in the several thousands of high fired pellets in the net pots where vegetative growth occurs in the grow tubes. The quality of the *Aqua-*

*Pod* bio-filter is in the ease of management. In any and all aquaponic systems the reservoir must be periodically cleaned and renewed without the total disruption of the bio-filter. Mismanagement of the reservoir can contribute to a bio-filter collapse and the subsequent death of the system aquaculture. With the *Aqua-Pod* this possibility is greatly diminished – if not eliminated all together – by the nature of management. When a plant plays out in the *Aqua-Pod* the net basket is removed, the high fired pebbles are taken out of the pot, cleaned, dried and replaced to the re-seeded net pot and returned to the system. With this technique there is a constantly renewed - clean - bio-filter medium without shocking the system.

**Exactly what are the water requirements for start-up & operation of the *Aqua-Pod*?**

Water requirements are very simple – clean sterilized water that has been treated to eliminate chlorine and chloramines. Do not use water from ponds, stream or rivers as they may have pathogens from the excretions of warm blooded mammals. At initial start-up establish a baseline pH, water clarity and TDS (total dissolved solids).

**The water pH has spiked to 8.9 during the fourth week since start-up. What can I do?**

The bio-filter is close to establishing itself. Help the system and the fish by pouring ½ cup of distilled white vinegar in the weir tank twice daily. Check pH for a .1 drop per day and increase or decrease vinegar dose to meet the required pH movement. Once the bio-filter is established the ph will fluctuate between 7.0 and 7.6. Monitor water clarity and TDS and compare to baseline findings.

**Water clarity has deteriorated in the fourth week since star-up. What can I do?**

Correct your pH and follow both pH and clarity closely. If the start-up fish population is mature and dense then a 1/3 change-out may be required. If clarity remains an issue as the pH approaches 7.5 check the TDS. If the TDS has not dropped from the 8.9 pH level proceed with another change-out.

**There are a number of Bio-Filter "starter" kits available on the internet. Can they be used?**

CRA R&D cannot recommend any of these products because we haven't used them and don't know if they work or not. It should be noted that there are products that claim to create a functioning bio-filter without fish involved at all! CRA R&D is very weary of, and reluctant to add, anything to our systems that is not fully understood, purely organic and known to be 100% safe for the aquaculture.

**What is the best fish to use for the system start-up?**

At CRA R&D we used "feeder" fish sold to aquarium enthusiast to feed larger species such as piranha. These fish are ¼" to ½" in size and we stocked the tanks at start-up with 100 of these fish and they performed well beyond our expectations. Once the original bio-filter was established the following 4 units were "jump" started from the first unit. In other words – it only required the establishment of the original bio-filter. If you have access to blue tilapia "fingerlings" (and it's legal in your locale) – ½" to 1" in length – purchase 100 and divide them between the 3 tanks. There are a number of fish options besides feeder fish and tilapia. It's suggested one reach out to the local aquaponic community to discover what is legal for their locale and what works best.

**What are the best plants to use for system start-up?**

During start-up operations – until the bio-filter is established – ammonia and nitrites are generated in high amounts and can stress the fish if not taken up by the vegetative roots. Unfortunately plants take up little ammonia and not much more in nitrites. Aloe, Cuban oregano and celery are what we call the "work horses" of any aquaponic system and would be the best choice for start-up. Any of the leafy greens can be seeded and installed as can tomatoes, cucumbers, basil and even okra but only in conjunction with the first three plants mentioned.

### How much do I feed the fish during start-up?

Feed the fish commercial food once daily during start-up and following the start-up. Feed enough to be eaten in 10 minutes and then, with a net, remove any uneaten food from the tank/pond surfaces. If there is duck weed or worms available feed the fish these items later in the day – in the evening. Both duck weed and worms are a good nutritional supplement and the fish love them.

### There isn't flow coming through all the flexible PVC to the grow tubes.

Check the Distribution Manifold and level if required. Adjust the ½" NPT barb fittings. There may be several that are screwed too far in.

### The sump is overflowing and the pump is not operating.

Check the level switch – raise it and determine the pump is operable. If the pump is running with the float switch manually raised adjust the float position by moving the wire ties to a satisfactory position. If the pump is not operating with the float raised by hand check the power supply at the GFI and energize if required. If GFI is engaged check the 15 AMP breaker supply.

### The GFI plug that the pump is on tripped. What should be done?

Find out what caused the Ground Fault Interruption to occur. In most cases (the only cases experienced at CRA R&D) there has been a heavy downpour causing the GFI to "trip". Wearing rubber soled shoes – NOT STANDING IN A PUDDLE OF WATER – reset the GFI. If there is water and no way to reset the GFI without standing in it – trip the 15 AMP source breaker, reset the GFI and then reset the 15 AMP source breaker.

## Hybrid Soil-Based Beds:

**Is it an absolutely necessity that hybrid soil-based be used in conjunction with the *Aqua-Pod*?**
Not necessarily, but it is highly recommended for several reasons. Not all plants do well in the aquaponic system. Some plants grow too large for the system and some plants simply don't grow in the systems while growing well in the soil-based beds. Bio-filter maintenance is much easier using soil-based hydroponics because fluctuating system parameters - fish population density and size - can be balanced through change-outs. One can assemble and operate grow tubes on a frame away from the *Aqua-Pod* structure but at greater cost and complexity while still limited to only those plants an aquaponic system will yield. There is a downside to growing soil-based hydroponics in that water usage increases from 2% to ≤6% of that used in industrial agriculture techniques. Unless water is of critical importance; utilizing soil-based hydroponics provides greater returns and flexibility for the operation.

**My celery is exhibiting stunted growth and central leaves are stunted.**
This may be an indication of calcium deficiency. Increase addition of horticulture hydrated lime to soil – gently. Research as required.

**My tomato plants lower leaves are tipped yellow and growth rate appears reduced.**
This may be an indication of potassium deficiency. Increase muriate of potash compounding to soil. Research as required.

**My Kale is exhibiting yellow blanched leaves with tints of yellow, orange and purple.**

This may be an indication of magnesium deficiency. Increase compounding of Epsom salts. Research as required.

**My plants are pale in color – not a vibrant green.**

This may be an indication of iron deficiency. Increase compounding of chelated iron. Research as required.

**My soil-based plants don't seem to be maturing at the proper rate.**

There may not be enough nitrates generated by the quantity and size of the fish population. If available increase composting of the soil. Add ¾" of sterilized cow manure to the bed keeping the manure away from the plant stem base(s). If necessary lay 2 or 4 beds fallow and observe.

**You discuss treating the municipal water to ensure the chlorines and chloramines are removed. What exactly removes these additives?**

Sodium Thiosulfate.

**You highly recommend AzaMax for pest control but you emphasize it be used without contacting the aquaculture. Why?**

The AzaMax MSDS (Material Safety Data Sheet) item 12 "Ecological Information" lists "Acute Fish Toxicity". It cites specifically rainbow trout but the warning should be taken seriously concerning any and all aquaculture.

**Are there other methods to achieve and assist in the control of pests?**

Yes there are a number of controls that can be used from the organic farmer's toolbox. Beneficial insects – of which the vast majority of insects are – maintained on the site will help. Plants grown that repel pests and soils treated with pest resistant additives – Spanish moss is one example - are helpful. We are researching several mixtures of dish soap, vinegar and water that are sprayed on plants to remove aphids and miner worms currently with mixed results.

**What are some basic guidelines concerning composting?**

Compost only items from vegetables and refrain from composting fruits. Never compost warm blooded animal wastes or leftovers. Compost filtered fish effluent solids and churn well. USDA requirements should be reviewed by visiting the "cfr organic composting" regulations through a web search portal. Compost can burn the plants so keep the compost away from the base stems if adding mid season.

**Operating the *Aqua-Pod* Farm/garden:**

**I forgot to feed the fish solid foods in the morning. What should I do?**

Feed the fish in the evening and clean uneaten food from the tank tops 10 minutes after feeding.

**Today the system pH is 7.5 but yesterday the pH was 7.8. Is that an issue?**

It's nothing to be overly concerned about as pH fluctuates. With pH changes consider temperature changes, rain water intrusion and any other additions since the pH was last tested. Have you added hydrated lime, Epson salts, chelated iron or muriate of potash to the systems? Has the TDS changing dramatically since last tested? Can you smell ammonia or rotting fish? If so then drag the tanks for a dead fish lying on the bottom. Is there an excess of organics in the tanks – leaves and such? Remove any – and all – organics in the tanks daily. Is the system over populated? Have fish for dinner. Are the tanks receiving adequate oxygen? Check that all air pumps and stones are operating properly.

**Today the system pH is 8.8 but yesterday the pH was 7.5. Is that an issue?**

Yes. Immediately perform a 30% change-out to the hydroponic beds. A change-out requires 30 minutes. Review the above items and correct any out of bound conditions. Blow-back all 3 tank returns to the weir tank. Confirm that the sump pump is operating properly and all supply tubes from the gravity manifold to the grow tubes are clear and running well (a daily requirement). Back fill the units with treated municipal water and continue to observe pH, TDS, water clarity and odors.

**The pH continues to rise. Today it was 9.1 up from 8.8 yesterday. What should be done?**

Immediately pursue a "clean & count" – see section "Operating the *Aqua-Pod* Garden – Annual Operations". This is a 3 hour operation. You may find the system overpopulated, dead fish or excessive organic materials in the system. Follow the instructions in this section to discover and correct the problem.

*The preceding two items have never been an issue at CRA R&D outside of the initial establishment of the bio-filter on the first unit "Pee-Wee". If proper attention has been observed – including the renewal of clean dry high fired pellets with each new seed planting in the system – these problems will not surface. Observe the systems DAILY (it takes 30 minutes or less) – pH, TDS, water clarity and odors. If necessary test for ammonia, nitrites and nitrates. Always maintain a balance of fish and plants. If necessary cull the population of fish by eating them. If plant stocks in the grow tubes are thin – get to seeding! In the mean time you'll have to balance the excess nitrates with change-outs to the soil-beds.*

*Approach the operation of the Aqua-Pod with this very basic tenet –*
*"There is zero tolerance of the senseless death of the aquaculture"!*

### When "topping" the sump – Does the water used need to be treated for chlorines and/or chloramines?

No is does not require treatment. The small amount of water required – 2 to 5 gallons – is not enough to require treatment of chlorine or chloramines.

### How do I know the system is properly "topped" up?

The system is properly "topped" when the tank/ponds are at the design level and overflowing to the weir which is, in turn, overflowing to the sump tank. Over "topping" can result in some loss of water and should be avoided. Over time the operator will become more knowledgeable and competent of correct "topping" procedures.

### Why are "change-outs" important and what significance do they play in the overall operation?

Water change-outs are important functions for several reasons. Change-outs are the best way to maintain a healthy bio-filter as variables fluctuate. Variables include fish sizes and population and plant density and size. Change-outs also permit one to grow plants with soil-based hydroponic methods increasing vegetable production and variety while maintaining water consumption at ≤6% that of industrial farming techniques.

### Plants and Vegetable Selection and Seeding:

### Why does the *Aqua-Pod* farm use both aquaponic and hydroponic growing methods?

Utilizing both methods permits a greater range of vegetable production and the ability to maintain, and tune, the bio-filter. It provides a significantly increased vegetable yield requiring a minimal increase in water usage.

**What are the major factors defining the difference between plants grown aquaponically and plants grown hydroponically?**

Mature plant size it the greatest factor. Though any plant can be propagated in the *Aqua-Pod* – usually with a greater success rate then soil-based techniques – some are simply too large and heavy for the net pots and need be transferred to the soil-beds when maturing. Examples of plants cultivated in the *Aqua-Pod* and transferred to soil beds are large tomatoes, carrots, broccoli, okra, Brussels sprouts, pole beans, large peppers, sunflowers, collards and rhubarb.

**I have been given a pesticide that I have heard works well. I don't know if it harmful to the fish in the system. How can I find out if it's harmful?**

All legitimately manufactured pesticides are required by law to provide a MSDS (material safety data sheet) with the product. The user of any pesticide, in any manner, is strongly urged to consult the MSDS prior to working with, and applying, the product. Section 12 of the MSDS lists "Toxicity" of the product and specifically toxicity to fish. If the product is listed as toxic to fish do not use it around the fish and ponds. Remove the plant, trim the roots, and treat downwind of the fish ponds. Return the plants to the system after the time indicated on the MSDS.

**I have a pesticide accepted and endorsed by OMRI (Organic Materials Review Institute). Does that mean the product is safe for fish and the aquaculture?**

NO! At CRA R&D we use, when required, a very effective product - AzaMax - which is endorsed by OMRI. In the accompanying MSDS it lists the product as "toxic to fish". When used the plants are removed from the system and treated downwind of the tank/ponds. The plants are returned to the system 3 hours following treatment.

**I have some plants I would like to grow that are not listed in the book. Why?**

At CRA R&D we simply haven't tried everything. With the *Aqua-Pod* system and farm you have extremely flexible and diverse methods of growing food. The major limiting factor in attempting to grow anything is taste, discipline and imagination. If the system is situated in the tropics and subtropics (as is the case with CRA R&D), in a greenhouse or with interior artificial lighting some issues with temperature or humidity may disqualify some plants. At CRA R&D our attempts to grow crocus (for saffron) found the plants failed due to high humidity. The heat of summer prevents the growing of parsley in the soil-based hydroponic beds. The best way to determine whether a plant will grow in your environment is through experimentation. You'll be surprised what can be grown with *Aqua-Pod* system and farm.

**Farm/garden Lay-out Details – CRA R&D:**

**I'm using one *Aqua-Pod* and I'm thinking of increasing my operation by adding another unit with the possibility of more units later. What are the major considerations for future growth?**

Since moving units about should be avoided (it can be done but pre-planning can prevent the need) the space between the units is the greatest importance. The units at CRA R&D are spaced a minimum distance that a wheelbarrow can be maneuvered between the units at the narrowest points. This applies to both interior based operations –

greenhouse and artificial lighting – and exterior operations. Exterior operations in the tropics and subtropics require a quality ground cover to keep native plants at bay and local pests out to the soil. Transfer piping layouts for feeding/watering of soil-based hydroponic beds need to be laid to anticipate additional runs as the farm size is increased. Soil-based beds need to be "bundled" in 8 barrels 2 wide x 4 length) with a wheelbarrow distance between the widths (distance between length runs of bundled beds can be 1' – enough to walk between). As previously mentioned the *Aqua-Pod* can be repositioned after construction and the soil bed/barrels can also be repositioned (two people using a hand truck) but planning well will prevent this. There is a drawing of the CRA R&D farm layout contained within this manual that will offer some guidance in layout for growth of the farm/garden.

**What are the prime qualities of a person – or of people - required to operate the *Aqua-Pod* and related farm?**

- A person operating any aquaponics system is committed to zero tolerance of the reckless destruction of the aquaculture. In short that means a person realizes and accepts that aquaponics is a 365 day per year obligation. If the operator cannot be available then another person must be brought in on a regular basis to manage the basic requirements of the farm – feeding the fish, topping the units daily and checking the mechanicals and electricals on a regular basis.

- Discipline is a requirement and following the instructions in this manual concerning items to attend - proper observations and testing of the water and conditions is a must. The ability to remain focused when adverse conditions arise and seek out knowledge and assistance early in a crisis.

- The love of fish and the requirement to sacrifice and eat the fish is an integral quality of a proper aquaponics operator.

- A fascination of plants and the subsequent growing, harvesting, preparing and eating that which is grown is important.

- Existing on this planet in a way that helps the world and all of its inhabitants while impacting it as little as possible is the most important prerequisite of a successful aquaponic operator.

**aqua.podcra@gmail.com**

# Aquaponics in a Changing World... Introducing the *Aqua-Pod*

## By Jim Gibson

*Food security at home and abroad is one of the most pressing issues of our time. The rapidly increasing effects of global climate change and the decreasing availability of water and fossil fuels are together projected to exert tremendous downward pressure on our global food supply. The development of aquaponics, a proven system for efficiently and symbiotically growing vegetables and fish together, may be one of the most important scientific and social innovations of the 21st century.*

*Aquaponics in a Changing World... Introducing the Aqua-Pod*
Take the guesswork out of gardening with this hands-on **construction & operations manual** to growing vegetables and fish together. Complete plans are combined with an introduction to the benefits of this exciting technology, tips for selecting plants and aquatic life, and detailed installation and maintenance instructions. Start small and grow your operation to any size to fit your needs.

*Aquaponics in a Changing World... Introducing the Aqua-Pod* provides step-by-step instructions for constructing a small-scale, highly efficient backyard or interior – greenhouse or artificial lighting - aquaponic farm. The system is specifically designed to produce the highest nutritional value using the least area, and the DIY approach relies on common components readily available at

most home improvement or hardware supply stores. The unique
addition of hybrid soil-based, aquaponics-fed, beds dramatically
increases the type and variety of produce that can be grown.
Unlike most of the books currently on the market which tend to offer
a broad overview of the technique, this hands-on, practical, concise
manual provides everything you need to know to get the *Aqua-Pod*
system up and running. Complete plans are combined with an
introduction to the benefits of this exciting technology, tips for
selecting plants and aquatic life, and detailed installation and
maintenance instructions.

*As the community and culture continue to move away from social
democracy – one person/one vote – and towards capital
manipulation – wealth devised government; aquaponics provides the
individual, the family and the community control over the most basic
of needs - food and nourishment for ourselves and our children.
There can be little debate about the fact our foods are being
manipulated to provide excessive profits for a very few. Aquaponics
"levels" the field is many ways.*

Jim Gibson is the founder and director of the Cyrson Ranch
Aquaponics Research & Development Center. After retiring from a
career as a Chief Engineer, U.S. Coast Guard licensed, he returned
home to apply his extensive knowledge of chemistry, hydraulics,
mechanics and thermodynamics to the development of a successful
aquaponics platform in response to the injustices he has witnessed in

his world travels and continues to observe in his daily existence. He is an accomplished carpenter, cabinet maker and a skilled electrician who has been tending gardens and growing food for most of his life.

*"Creating food with fish poop isn't all that attractive to the uneducated – both those uneducated regarding the science of aquaponics and those uneducated about the methods of production of their current food stream. I am certain - I repeat – I am certain that aquaponic production will not only become viable but that it may be one of the most important scientific and social innovations of the 21st century. If I am over passionate, please forgive me, but I suggest that aquaponic technology may well feed the human race at some point in the not too distant future. In 2008, when I entered into aquaponic research & development I was of the belief aquaponics would achieve a solid footing worldwide in 50 to 75 years. I now suspect it will be a major component of vegetable and protein*

*production in the next 15 to 25 years. It will depend on the weather and the rapidly increasing affects of global climate change and the decreasing availability of water and fossil fuels. It will also depend on whether **we** know the process and can deliver on it. We **must** teach ourselves and our children these methods and our children **must** leave this knowledge to all for all times."*

**aqua.podcra@gmail.com**

www.ingramcontent.com/pod-product-compliance
Lightning Source LLC
Chambersburg PA
CBHW060449290526
45791CB00001B/41